PARTNERSHIP IN PRACTICE

This book is the second in a series published in association with CEDR

Series Editor: *Robin Lovelock*

Already published:

CHANGING PATTERNS OF MENTAL HEALTH CARE
a case study in the development of local services

Jackie Powell and Robin Lovelock

Forthcoming titles:

VISUAL IMPAIRMENT: SOCIAL SUPPORT
recent research in context

Robin Lovelock

DISABILITY: BRITAIN IN EUROPE
an evaluation of UK participation in
    tn the HELIOS programme (1988-1991)
                    (provisional title)

Robin Lovelock and Jackie Powell

Partnership in Practice

The Children Act 1989

Edited by
ANN BUCHANAN

Avebury

Aldershot • Brookfield USA • Hong Kong • Singapore • Sydney

Published by
Avebury
Ashgate Publishing Limited
Gower House
Croft Road
Aldershot
Hants GU11 3HR
England

Ashgate Publishing Company
Old Post Road
Brookfield
Vermont 05036
USA

Typeset by
Kathleen Fedouloff
44 Rosemont Road
London W3 9LY
081-993 8258

British Library Cataloguing in Publication Data
Partnership in Practice: Children Act, 1989
– (CEDR Series)
  I. Buchanan, Ann II. Series
  362.7

ISBN 1 85628 561 8

Printed and Bound in Great Britain by
Athenaeum Press Ltd, Newcastle upon Tyne.

Contents

v

Figures and tables

List of contributors

Alton Family Resource Centre

Kish Bhatti-Sinclair, Lecturer in Social Work Studies, University of Southampton

Jill Blanchard, Practitioner, Hampshire Social Services Department

Dr Ann Buchanan, Lecturer in Social Work Studies, University of Southampton

The Dolphin Project– young people being looked after by local authorities

Adrian Faupel, Senior Educational Psychologist, Hampshire

Ruth Forrester, formerly Team Manager, Hampshire Social Services

Gill Farmer, Practitioner, Hampshire Social Services Department,

Jan Goodwin, Practitioner, Hampshire Social Services Department

Carol Hayden, Researcher, Social Services Research and Information Unit (SSRIU), University of Portsmouth

Rob Hutchinson, Deputy Director, Hampshire Social Services Department

Shirley Jackson, Family Rights Group, London

Diana King, Hampshire Social Services Training Department

Elizabeth Marks, Researcher, University of Southampton

Hazel Osborn, Lecturer in Social Work Studies, University of Southampton

Jon Philpot, Implementation Officer, Children Act, Hampshire Social Services Department

Jackie Powell, Lecturer in Social Work Studies, University of Southampton

Colin Pritchard, Professor of Social Work, University of Southampton

Geoff Poulton, SCOPE and University of Southampton

Gwen James, A Voice for the Child in Care, London

Sylvia Sleeman, Lecturer in Social Work Studies, University of Southampton

Dr Christine Smalley, Paediatrician, Community Child Health, Southampton

Nina Swarup, Researcher, Social Services Research and Information Unit (SSRIU), University of Portsmouth

Vaughan Tudor Williams, Advisor Children's Homes, Hampshire Social Services Department

Daphne Walder, Facilitator, Dolphin Project, University of Southampton

Jackie Walton, Practitioner, Hampshire Social Services Department,

Ann Wheal, Facilitator, Dolphin Project, University of Southampton

Acknowledgements

In September 1992, 150 parents, young people who had been looked after, volunteers and professionals came to a conference at the University of Southampton in September 1992 to discover what they felt working in partnership under the Children Act 1989 meant. This book would not have been possible without their endeavours. It would also not have been possible without those who went to the additional labour of writing up their contributions.

We are particularly indebted to Smith's Charity whose generous donation enabled us to fund the conference at a price which enabled all to attend, and to the Baring Foundation who funded the original work of the Dolphin Project.

Hopefully this book will convince others that much can be learnt by bringing together in one gathering representatives of all the partners who in one way or another have a role under the Children Act 1989. If this book encourages others to organize similar events it will have achieved its aim.

As editor I would particularly like to thank Dr Jane Aldgate, who agreed to comment on the original script, the Family Rights Group, Jo Gooderham of Avebury, Jackie Powell and Robin Lovelock, and all my colleagues in the Department of Social Work Studies who did not complain when I bullied them for their contributions, as well as Frankie Lambert and all the administrative staff for their help at the conference.

Ann Buchanan
September 1993

Part One
INTRODUCTION

1 Partnership and the Children Act 1989

Ann Buchanan

The Children Act 1989 is 'the most comprehensive and far-reaching reform of child law... in living memory' (Mackay, 1988). What the Children Act does is to bring together under one statute legislation relating to children and families which had previously been scattered across the statute books. But much more than that, the Act also seeks to legislate for a major change in attitudes and practice as it relates to child care. Central to this change is the concept of the parties to the Act *'working in partnership'*.

Background

The thinking behind the Children Act 1989 began with the publication of the 1984 report of the House of Commons Select Committee on young people in care, which highlighted that there were eight or more pieces relating to the 'public law' aspects of child care; that is where social service departments intervened on behalf of children, and a further twelve or more statutes relating to the private law aspects of child care; that is all those aspects which did not involve the local authorities. The sheer bulk of the law and its complexities, as well as the feeling that it did not produce an acceptable balance between the welfare of the child and the integrity of the family, was also highlighted by this Committee. One of its main recommendations was:

The time has arrived – indeed it arrived some time ago – for a thorough-going review of the body of statute law, regulations and judicial decisions relating to children, with a view to the production of a simplified and coherent body of law comprehensible not only to those operating it but also those affected by its operation. It is not just to make life easier for practitioners that the law must be sorted out; it is for the sake of justice that the legal framework of the child and the care system must be rationalized.

The 1985 Review of Child Care Law and the 1987 White Paper (DHSS, 1985) followed quickly on the heels of the first report.

The Act that followed was indeed comprehensive, more user-friendly than previous legislation, and more importantly struck a more equitable balance between the rights of the child and those of his/her parents.

Part 1 of the Act is largely devoted to how children and parents should be viewed under the law:

> A child's welfare shall be paramount... the court shall have regard to: the ascertainable wishes and feelings of the child concerned.
>
> (Children Act 1989: section 1)

as well as the concept of 'parental responsibility' that is:

> all the rights, duties, powers, responsibilities and authority which by law a parent of a child has in relation to the child and his property.
>
> (Children Act 1989: section 3)

Part II incorporates these principles in the 'private law' aspects of the legislation especially where children come before the courts following their parents' divorce actions. Part III introduces a further principle:

> It shall be the duty of every local authority...to safeguard and promote the welfare of children within their area who are in need and as far as consistent with that duty to promote the upbringing of such children by their families.
>
> (Children Act 1989: section 17 (a) and (b))

Part IV and V outline the conditions whereby a child may be compulsorily removed from his family, and the care that the local authority must provide in these circumstances. Following the principle that children are best brought up in their families, the grounds for compulsory separation are limited:

> A court may only make a care order or supervision order if it is satisfied:

(a) that the child concerned is suffering, or is likely to suffer, significant harm: and

(b) that the harm or likelihood of harm is attributable to :

    (i) the care given to the child or likely to be given to him if the order were not made, not being what it would be reasonable to expect a parent to give to him; or

    (ii) the child's being beyond parental control.

(Children Act 1989: section 31 (2))

Partnership – what does it mean?

Although the word 'partnership' does not appear in the Act itself, working in partnership is a central principle in the provision of services for children and families envisaged by, and a recurring theme in the many volumes of regulations and guidance associated with the Act. In this way the Act was unusual in that it was trying to legislate a major change in attitudes as well as practice.

The concept of partnership is first introduced in *The Care of Children – Principles and Practice*. This was one of the initial volumes on guidance brought out by the Department of Health before the actual implementation of the Act.

> The very fundamental changes in thinking and in policy practice and terminology which the implementation of the Act will demand, make this seem a particularly important time to publish a set of basic principles ... partnership, participation, choice, openness, parental responsibility and every child's need for both security and family links are some of the major themes which are common to the principles and to the legislation....
>
> (DOH, 1989: The Care of Children)

This guidance however, poses a dilemma. What does the term mean? Does partnership exist or is it simply empty rhetoric? Who should work in partnership, when and for what purpose and how do you do it? Do we for example all mean the same thing by 'partnership under the Children Act 1989'.

The vagueness of the definition for 'parental responsibility' suggests the legislators did not find it easy to define the new principles. It would have been considerably more difficult to give a legal definition to the concept of partnership.

However, within the volumes of guidance and regulation, efforts are made to clarify the term. The principle of continuing parental responsibility which can only be severed in the case of death or adoption, necessitates an ongoing relationship with parents. No longer can the local authority take over 'parental rights' when a child comes to be looked after in public care. Even in the case of a Care Order the local authority only shares parental responsibility with the parents. The first idea is therefore that 'partnership' is something that happens between professionals in child care and parents when services are required for a 'child in need', that is a child whose health or welfare may be in jeopardy under Part III of the Act.

> The development of a working partnership with parents is usually the most effective route to providing supplementary or substitute care for children. Measures which antagonize, alienate, undermine or marginalize parents are counterproductive.
>
> (DOH, 1989: *The Care of Children*)

But central to the Children Act is also the idea that the local authorities should not be the only providers. Involved in this partnership to support children and families are a range of both of statutory and voluntary groups, amongst these may be parents working in partnership with other parents in self help groups:

> 4.13: In each area there will be a wide range of providers... different departments in local authorities... voluntary organizations, self-help or community groups.
>
> (DOH, 1991: R&G Vol 2)

In Volume Two of regulations and guidance, the concept of partnership is further expanded. Here it suggests the important principle that children should be part of this partnership, and that all the parties need information if they are to be 'partners' to any decision making.

> 2.28: Partnership requires informed participation. The Act therefore requires that parents and children must be consulted during the decision-making process and notified of the outcome... The Act emphasises that where possible children should participate in decision-making about their future well being... such participation requires that a child is provided with relevant information and is consulted at every stage in the process of decision-making.
>
> (DOH, 1991: R&G Vol 2)

Partnership with parents and children is also recommended as a key concept in child protection:

> 1.4: Local authorities have, under the Children Act 1989, a general duty to safeguard and promote the welfare of children within their area who are in need and so far as is consistent with that duty to promote the upbringing of such children by their families. As parental responsibility is retained notwithstanding any court orders, short of adoption, local authorities must work in partnership with parents, seeking court orders when compulsory action is indicated in the interests of the child but only when

this is better for the child than working with the parents under voluntary arrangements...

(DOH, 1991: Working Together)

Finally, there is also the direction that working in partnership, or inter-disciplinary and inter-agency co-operation, should be something that happens between professional agencies for the welfare of the specific children. For example where a child has disabilities (DOH, 1991: R&G Vol 6, Chapter 6, para 6.1-6.5) as well as in the case of child protection:

> 1.8. Agencies should ensure that staff who are concerned with the protection of children from abuse understand that this assumption in the Act of a high degree of co-operation between parents and local authorities requires a concerted approach to inter-disciplinary and inter-agency working.

(DOH, 1991: Working Together)

The background to the Partnership Principle

For almost twenty years the issue of state intervention into family life has been at the centre of media attention. On the one hand were the failures of the state to protect children from abuse, (DOH, 1982, 1991: *Child Abuse – Study of Inquiry Reports 1973-1981 and 1980-1989*) and on the other hand what was felt to be over-zealous intervention by the state in Cleveland (Butler Sloss, 1988). Studies such as 'The needs of parents' (Pugh & De'Ath, 1985) demonstrated that the confidence of parents was undermined by the increasing number of child care experts with whom parents came into contact through their children. Parents were seen as falling into two camps: either they were 'good enough' and did not need any help from the state, or they were 'deficient' and needed the local authority to take over their parental rights.

However, spearheaded by the Partnership Studies from the National Children's Bureau, evidence grew during the 1980's that in centres where professionals 'worked with parents' rather than 'did things to them', effective relationships between professionals and parents could be created, especially where these relationships were built on notions of partnership and mutual respect and these relationships benefited the child. (De'Ath & Pugh, 1985-6, Pugh et al., 1987)

At the same time other groups were demonstrating that parent involvement, the use of written agreements, and partnership between parents and professionals could not only enhance a child's development and health (Elfer & Gatiss, 1990), but lead to more appropriate child care planning, better decisions and more parental co-operation. (Aldgate, 1989)

During this period another milestone was struck when in 1985, Lord Scarman reached a decision in the House of Lords on the Gillick Case.

Parental rights are derived from parental duty and exist so long as they are needed for the protection of the person and the property of the child... parental right yields to the child's right to make his own decisions when he reaches a sufficient understand and intelligence to be capable of making up his own mind on the matter requiring decision.

(*Gillick* v *West Norfolk and Wisbech Area Health Authority* 1986)

From this decision flowed the idea that children and young people of sufficient age and understanding' should be involved in the decision-making process and become, with or without their parents, 'partners' to the decisions. This finding, which became a central tenet of the Children Act, was reinforced by the United Nations Convention on the Rights of the Child (UN, 1989) and its later ratification in the United Kingdom, in December 1991.

Linked into these developments has been a growing movement of consumer participation in all areas of service provision, disability, learning disability, mental health, elderly(Beeforth et al., 1990), and child care (Buchanan et al., 1993). Consumer involvement is, of course, an essential component for developing quality services in a world which is increasingly becoming market-orientated, as local authorities develop care management strategies along the purchaser/provider split advocated by the White Paper and the National Health Service and Community Care Act 1990. Consumer involvement is also especially important in groups who may not have had a voice in the past and may have been severely disempowered as a result.

The inspiration for this book

The fact that one of the key principles to the Children Act 1989 is not in itself mentioned in the Act suggests, apart from possible difficulties of definition, that there is an expectation that partnership or the working relationships between the respective parties will to some extent, evolve in practice. In September 1992, nearly one year after the implementation of the Act, some 150 people who were in one way or another connected in receiving or supplying services under the Act, came together in Southampton to say what they felt was meant by 'Partnership and the Children Act 1989', and how they felt it was working out in practice. Amongst this group were representatives of parent organizations, young people who had been looked after by the local authority, child care professionals, educationalists, doctors, health workers, social workers, teachers, residential workers, foster carers, play group leaders and youth group leaders. This book is the result of their labours.

The first chapters are written by representatives of the key actors in

8

the partnership contract; the parents, represented by Shirley Jackson of the Family Rights Group; the child, represented by the Dolphin Group; young people who had been looked after by local authorities and who had taken part in the author's research project which elicited their views on the Children Act 1989; and finally the local authority provider represented by Rob Hutchinson Acting Director of Hampshire Social Services. The second part of the book highlights some key research on partnership projects relating to the Children Act and hears from key specialists in the field describing how they work in partnership under the Children Act. Finally, there are some practical examples of how workers in Hampshire have put the partnership principle into practice in their day to day work in a variety of settings.

Summary

The Children Act 1989 poses a dilemma. Partnership is highlighted as a key concept in implementing the Act, but the term does not appear in the Act itself nor is it defined in regulations and guidance. The volumes of regulations and guidance on the Act suggest that partnership should be a way of working between parents and professionals, professionals and children, parents and other support agencies, when a child is 'in need'. The following definition which comes from the Partnership Papers of the National Children's Bureau gives us a possible starting point in exploring the meaning of partnership under the Children Act 1989.

> A working relationship that is characterized by a shared sense of purpose, mutual respect and the willingness to negotiate. This implies a sharing of information, responsibility, skills, decision making and accountability.
>
> (Pugh et al., 1987)

But what this means in practice will become clearer in the following chapters.

(References for this and all subsequent chapters are collated at the end of the book)

9

Part Two
THE PARTNERS

2 The voice of the family

Shirley Jackson

Introduction

This paper presenting the views of the Family Rights Group, represents the voice of the family. It will focus on four main areas; firstly, it will describe the work of the Family Rights Group (FRG); secondly, it will give a few thoughts on what FRG means by partnership; thirdly, what they hoped for in the Children Act; and fourthly, what they have found in practice. The final section will end with a few thoughts on how things can be improved.

Who are the Family Rights Group?

We are a national charity based in the North-East of London. We have a staff of ten including social workers, solicitors, a training manager, administration and finance workers. We run a national advice service for family members and professionals on child protection, care, and related issues under the Children Act 1989. We also organize courses on child care law and practice and we respond to central and local government initiatives on child care law and family services. We were very involved in the consultation process before the Act was finalized.

The aim of our organization is to promote a family and child care service that builds on the strengths within families and seeks to make available to all families the respect and resources that make possible the difficult task of rearing children. The information I shall be using has come from our advice service, from comments passed to us via participants on our courses and at other meetings of professionals, and from a very exciting conference which we held in the summer of 1992. At this conference, which was organized jointly with the Department of Health, we brought together a number of users of the child protection procedures who expressed their views on the way those procedures had impinged on their families and ways in which they felt that process could be improved.

What do we mean by partnership?

There are numerous definitions of 'partnership'. One of the problems is that the term can mean quite different things to different people. In this section, rather than choose another possibly misleading definition , let me quote from a letter I received recently in our advice service. By way of background, we had been approached by a mother who was feeling excluded from decision making about her son who was in care. I had written to the social worker concerned relaying this information to her. In reply she wrote:

> Working in partnership is not something I have adopted from October 15th 1991 but it is the way I have always worked whenever possible.

However, it was clear that this social worker and her client had very different ideas about what it meant to work in partnership.

Unfortunately, this is not an isolated occurrence. Such mismatch of understanding is a common feature of our advice service. Partnership is not just inviting someone to a meeting, it is far more than that. The essence of partnership is sharing. It is showing respect for one another, it is the right to information, accountability, with each person seen as having something to contribute, it is the sharing of power and decisions being made jointly. Volume 3(2), para 13 in the guidance on the Children Act says in relation to the provision of accommodation:

> The parents contribute their experience and knowledge of the child to the decision. The local authority brings a capacity to provide services, to coordinate the contribution of other agencies and to plan for and review the child's needs.
>
> (DOH, 1991: G&R Vol 3)

There is clearly here an intention for shared power, common respect and an understanding of the different but equally important roles undertaken by the family and the local authority. How often is this true in our practice?

It is important to be clear about what is not partnership. It is not equal power and it never can be, but it is about empowerment, about families having sufficient information to be able to understand and contribute to planning and having some power to influence the outcome. Many families we advise would be happy with that much.

What we hoped for from the Children Act 1989

In this section I will outline what the Family Rights Group hoped for from the implementation of the Children Act. I would first like to lay to rest the old adage that parents' and children's interests are at odds. I quote:

> A distinction is often drawn between the interests of children and the interests of their parents. In the great majority of families, including those who are for one reason or another in need of social services, this distinction does not exist. The interests of the children are best served by their remaining with their families and the interests of their parents are best served by allowing them to undertake their natural and legal responsibility to care for their own children. Hence the focus of effort should be to enable and assist parents to discharge those responsibilities. Even where a child has to spend some time away from home, every effort should be made to maintain and foster links between the child and his/her family to care for the child in partnership with, rather than in opposition to, his/her parents and to work towards his/her return home.
>
> (DHSS, 1985)

This may sound like a quote from some Family Rights Group publication. They are our sentiments but they are not our words. It comes from the government's consultative document which preceded the White Paper and the Children Act itself.

Family Rights Group Hopes for the Children Act 1989

- More involvement in decision-making processes
- More involvement in child protection procedures
- Better anti-racist practice
- Involvement of users in service design and monitoring
- Improved contact arrangements for families
- Positive action to improve re-unification work
- More consideration of the wider family and community

15

The Family Rights Group wanted a number of outcomes from the implementation of the Act. We wanted families to feel and be involved in decision-making. We wanted families to be empowered in the child protection process. After all, 85% of children who are subject to a child protection case conference remain at home and, as the main caretakers, the parents clearly need to be involved in all aspects of the decision-making process from start to finish.

We hoped for better anti-racist practice; for example, more attention being given to ensuring that the black minority ethnic communities are involved in consultation on service provision so that family support services are the ones they want to use. We also hoped for recruitment of more black staff, day carers and foster carers, for information in different languages, for non-Eurocentric assessments and more than just lip service paid to issues of race and culture.

We also wanted involvement of users in the design of services to ensure that services would meet their own needs, and user involvement in monitoring and review of service provision – asking people what they feel about the services they have received.

We wanted more notice to be taken of the research on contact with families, and for continuing contact to be encouraged and promoted as outlined in the Act. We wanted continuing contact to be a matter of course, and only terminated in the few extreme cases where it would not serve the long-term interests of the child, and we hoped that there would be a rethink on permanency planning philosophy. We also hoped for a more positive attitude to families, to reunification, to enabling families to stay together, and we wanted the wider family to be given much more consideration. Partnership is not just about parental involvement – it is about family involvement.

What the Family Rights Group found

By September 1992, some of our hopes for the Children Act had been realized. Local authorities no longer had the power to terminate contact between children and parents without recourse to the court and in only one circumstance was a local authority found attempting to violate this new right. We had also found most local authorities had a clear complaints procedure. These were up and running and most local authorities had leaflets explaining families' rights. Many local authorities also now have leaflets for family members on the child protection procedures.

Realities of the Children Act 1989

- Some general changes: law on contact improved, complaints procedures in place, more parents participating in child protection conferences

- Examples of innovative practice

HOWEVER

- DATA syndrome: 'Doing All That Already'
- Families still not involved in decision-making process, often a lack of information on procedures
- Contact with families not being maintained or being promoted especially in cases where reunification was unlikely
- Relatives still overlooked or treated as second best
- Section 27: whereby other agencies such as Housing can be involved, was not being used.

Today, many authorities are inviting parents into the whole of child protection conferences. In their introductory information many authorities are now recommending that people bring along a friend or representative, some even specify that people can bring their solicitor.

There are areas of innovative practice. One London borough consulted its users on what sort of services they would like to see in their area. Emanating from this day was a joint training course for professionals and service users on written agreements which hoped to develop a better working relationship between social workers and clients.

Some other areas were looking at ways of involving families in the decision making around child protection issues prior to the conference stage.

One authority had used a member of the Grandparents' Federation as an independent person on their complaints procedure and they had had to face up to some of the challenges this has brought.

However, the overwhelming feeling from our advice service is that there is still a great need for a change in attitude amongst social workers and managers. As epitomized by my initial quotation from a particular social worker's letter, many social workers and managers seem to have the DATA syndrome – Doing All That Already, but we have had cases from all over the country including those discussed, where this is obviously not so. Also, worryingly, we have picked up from courses and other meetings that, in some areas, the Act has been dismissed as a parents' charter which puts children at risk, and workers are looking for ways of getting round the Act, rather than implementing it.

For many families, the feeling is that very little has changed in the day-to-day way they are dealt with. Let me give you a few examples from our advice service. Firstly, two children were 'in accommodation' with no written agreement or plan for their stay. At a child protection conference, it was recommended that the two children be returned home from accommodation. The day after this conference a further meeting was held, chaired by the area manager. He started the meeting with a list of reasons why the department was not happy for the children to go home. After a few heated exchanges, the area manager resorted to saying that he would be happy for the whole matter to be decided in court. Of course, by the time this situation would have reached court, the chances of the children being returned home would be negligible. The family not surprisingly were aggrieved that the second meeting could effectively negate the recommendations of the official child protection meeting.

Secondly, after some intervention by Family Rights Group, a small child was placed with grandparents rather than remaining in a stranger foster home. The parents had regular but supervised and specified contact. The health visitor phoned the mother but erroneously thought that she had phoned the grandparents' phone number. The social worker and team leader visited the family immediately and accused them of breaking the contact arrangement, saying that they could not work with them if they were going to be so dishonest. When eventually they found that the Health Visitor did not even have the grandparents' phone number they realized that a mistake had been made. It was not the fact that they were investigated that worried the family. It was the way in which they investigated. It was assumed the family were guilty before asking them anything. It was assumed they would be lying. Even on finding that they had made a genuine mistake there was no element of apology.

Thirdly, an aunt phoned the social services department as her brother (the child's father) had been asked to contact social services with plans for the child as they were concerned about him. He was particularly asked to contact them with reference to anyone else in the family who could look after the child. The aunt was offering the child a home but was very abruptly told by the social worker that it was none of her business and they could only talk with the father.

These cases are not presented as horror stories but as examples of the many things we hear through our telephone advice line. These really do lead me to question whether there has been a change of attitude in some areas of social workers' practice.

Specific areas

The following outlines just a few specific issues where we hoped for change but have found worrying developments under the Act.

Involvement in decision making

Families still feel they are not adequately involved in the decision-making process about their children. One woman who was in contact with the FRG only found out about a review of her daughter's case from the daughter herself a few days beforehand. On another occasion, a social worker told a parent that in their borough they did not allow representatives into reviews. It was later found out that it was an individual chair's decision as to whether or not a representative was admitted.

Despite the legislation, there have been a number of situations where parents were full participants in a meeting but they did not receive the minutes. It is still very rare for parents to receive minutes of meetings at which they did not or were not allowed to attend.

There still seems to be a considerable lack of information given to people about child protection procedures. In one case a woman was given no information about the purpose of child protection procedures. When the chair was asked if he could brief her he was clearly amazed that this could be part of his role and consequently failed to give her any useful information.

Contact

Another very important area is 'contact' with families. This is a sadly neglected area of work, and one wonders how much training social workers receive about contact? On my own Certificate in Qualification in Social Work course, keeping in touch with families of young people who were in care, was relegated to one seminar in an optional course, and I do not recall reading or discussing anything about its importance, nor hearing about the research background and some of the difficulties than can occur and yet be overcome.

But for families it is crucial, and it is often where difficulties between family members, social workers and foster carers arise. The Dartington researchers found in their studies *Lost in Care* (Millham et al., 1986) and *Access Disputes in Child Care* (Millham et al., 1989) that contact is essential if children are to return home. Research has also shown that contact is important for giving a sense of identity when children are not returning home. From recent experience in our advice service, it appears that not much has changed. Difficulties between carers and families always reflect badly on the families and contact is often cut as a result. It is still commonplace for contact to be stopped at the time of placement 'to let the child settle'. We need to acknowledge that disturbed behaviour exhibited by a child after contact may not be unreasonable and that contact should not necessarily be curbed because of it. Contrary to the Act and guidance on it, factors such as distance, money, and social environment are still reasons for contact not working, and we need to think more creatively about how to make contact arrangements work. We also find that contact is often supervised and restrictive when there is no real reason for it. The Act is very clear that it is the local authority's responsibility to promote and maintain contact between children and their families and this includes the wider family and communities from which they have come, not just their parents. We do not find this to be the case.

It is still a very common experience that contact is cut prior to a Freeing Order for adoption or adoption application. This makes the decision, by the time it gets to court a fait accompli. Recent research has shown that 97% of freeing applications by the local authority, are successful (Lowe et al., 1991). Despite all the evidence on the benefits of continued contact, it is rarely encouraged post adoption. It appears that local authorities are not promoting and encouraging contact, unless there is a very imminent prospect of reunification.

Reunification

At the Family Rights Group we see little evidence of greater efforts being made to support and help families' care for their own children. We see a dogged determination to implement the view that, after a short period when families are expected to get their act together sometimes with a very supportive programme but very often no help at all, they are quickly dismissed in favour of permanent substitute families usually leading to adoption. The argument we hear is often about lack of resources. Clearly lack of resources is a great problem and more resources would be very welcome, but a change of attitude does not require more resources. We are disturbed that reunification work still plays a very poor second to the specialisms of fostering and adoption in the allocation of resources. This is despite the requirements in the Act that:

> It should be the general duty of every local authority, so far is consistent with that duty to promote the upbringing of such children by their families by providing a range and level of services appropriate to those children's needs.
>
> (Children Act 1989 : section 17)

and

> Any local authority looking after a child shall make arrangements to enable him to live with
> (a) a parent of the child or someone with parental responsibility or
> (b) a relative, friend or other person connected with him unless that would not be reasonably practicable or consistent with his welfare.
>
> (Children Act 1989: section 23(6)

For anyone still in doubt as to the intentions of the Act, the following quote from the Department of Health publication, *Principles and Practice in Regulations and Guidance.* (DOH, 1989) gives just two of their principles of good child care practice:

There are unique advantages for children in experiencing normal family life in their own birth family and every effort should be made to preserve the child's home and family links.

(DOH, 1989: P&P)

and

Admission to public care by virtue of a compulsory order is in itself a risk to be balanced against others so also is the accommodation of a child by a local authority.

(DOH, 1989: P&P)

These risks should be weighed up more carefully before advocating fostering and adoption above reunification work.

The use of relatives as carers

FRG finds that more relatives are being used as carers for children than before the Children Act 1989. However, there are still numerous occasions where relatives put themselves forward as carers and are either ignored or have to undergo an assessment before placement which does not take into account the fact that they are only wanting to be assessed for this child. This leads to unnecessary and detrimental delay in placement of the child within the family.

A very worrying trend has also developed with regard to payment of relatives as carers. There have been a number of cases where the relatives are not made any payment, or they have been paid at a lower rate, and in some cases even as low as income support levels. This is a worrying trend which is also of concern to the National Foster Care Association.

Section 27

Finally, there is a much neglected section of the Act which we think could be used in many more cases to enable the families to stay together. This is section 27 of The Children Act, the ability of social services departments to request other departments and agencies to provide services. We are finding that many local authorities are not using this provision, especially in relation to housing. A number of families are finding that they are not being re-united with their children due to housing need and social services departments are not using their power under section 27 to request housing departments or housing associations to provide suitable accommodation. Unfortunately, recent case law has determined that section 27 cannot be used in unitary authorities, (*R* v *Tower Hamlets*, 1992) but is still available to non-unitary authorities, for example county councils, where it has been used more successfully, for example in relation to housing (*R v North Avon* 1993).

21

Obviously there are many other areas of our work which touch on partnership, but I would now like to turn to some of the ways that might improve things for families.

What you can do about it

Firstly, the most importance message from our advice service and the Department of Health Users Day is that people feel they do not have adequate information. People need leaflets about child protection procedures, and they need to be given them as a matter of course. We are suggesting to all local authorities that they purchase our guide jointly written with the NSPCC about child protection procedures and that, with each case, they discuss with the family what the procedures will mean for family members. When children become 'looked after', families should be given written information about their legal position, review system and so on. Information on complaints procedures and review systems are required by the legislation. People need information about the complaints procedure and they need to be given it as soon as they request it rather than being fobbed off in the hope that they will forget about the difficulties or it can be dealt with at a lower level. The complaints procedure was designed for people to have easy access to it and obviously, unless they know it exists and how to use it, it is a useless part of the legislation. People need to be given information about advice services on Family and Children's Rights and they also need the names of local support groups and agencies.

Information is power, and sharing is therefore an easy way of empowering families. It is also crucial that family members are given minutes of meetings, not doctored or summarized edits, but the same level of information that other professionals get. In fact, the Children Act Regulations require information to be given in writing after a review. They also require written plans to be given for children being looked after by the local authority, and written agreements incorporating the plan to be made in certain circumstances.

Secondly, I would say, encourage complaints. Do not be afraid of the loss of power or the accountability. People need to feel that they can complain efficiently and effectively. One important issue raised by the users who attended our Department of Health day, was that they found social workers made very quick judgements about situations and were not prepared to change their minds. Let us see the complaints procedure as a tool for negotiation, not as an indictment for failure. Let us also learn from the outcome of complaints. Following on from that, let us encourage local support groups. Local authorities can help in co-ordinating them as long as they don't dominate them.

Finally, in establishing your policies, why not ask users? It is easier to consult users about policies, services and monitoring if you have a body like a local support group which can discuss its response. In Norfolk and Newcastle, such consultation has become commonplace with the local authorities concerned. I talk with families all the time at FRG, but I would not have known that information was the main thing that they wanted in relation to child protection procedures until our day with the Department of Health. So do not assume that you know what people want, but ask them.

In summary, the message from families who have come to the Family Rights Group, is that there are examples of good practice and some social workers and managers are really seeking to work in partnership with them. But the time has not yet come to be complacent or overly self-congratulatory – there is still a long way to go before families can say they are partners with the local authorities.

3 The voice of the child

REPORT BY YOUNG PEOPLE ON THE CHILDREN ACT 1989

THE DOLPHIN PROJECT
facilitated by Ann Wheal and Daphne Walder

During the summer of 1992, forty-five young people aged between 11-19 being looked after in three local authorities, met to give their views on the changes that had taken place under the Children Act 1989. There were six groups of young people and each group met for three sessions of two hours. Discussions centred around a range of topics related to the Children Act and young people were encouraged to raise other issues that were important to them. The full findings from this work which became known as the Dolphin Project, are reported elsewhere (Buchanan et al., 1993). Eleven young people from this project felt sufficiently strongly about the issues raised to travel to Southampton to take part in the partnership conference. At the conference the young people took questions from the floor and some of the issues raised by the young people were presented in a report. This chapter outlines the central themes of this report, in particular the qualities of a professional working partnership with a young person.

One of the key principles of the Children Act 1989 is:

...a court shall have regard in particular to:
a)   the ascertainable wishes and feelings of the child concerned (considered in the light of his age and understanding);

(Children Act 1989: section 1(3))

Closely related to this is the concept of working in partnership with young people:
One of the key principles of the Children Act is that responsible

24

authorities should work in partnership with the parents of a child who is being looked after and also with the child himself where he is of sufficient age and understanding, provided that this approach will not jeopardize his welfare. A second closely related principle is that parents and children should participate in the decision-making process...

The child's views should be sought in discussion with the child.
(DOH, 1991: G&R Vol 4.)

If, however, young people are to share in the decision-making process they need information.

What the young people knew about the Children Act

Most young people in the project had not heard of the Children Act. Although some authorities had special information leaflets and guides for them, very few young people had seen them. Young people were desperate for information which they needed in order to make decisions and plans about their lives. This was particularly important for those reaching care-leaving age. Information is an essential prerequisite to a partnership relationship.

> I had never heard of The Children Act, so when I got your letter I went to the library to find out what it was.

> The Children Act has been brought in... and the children did not know about it.

> Social workers... have they heard about it?

> I want to read the script of the Children Act from start to finish.

> I wish there were a few more meetings (like Dolphin). This has only given us the basis of the information we need. I think we should have meetings like this perhaps all the time.

> I have found out...things (since joining the Dolphin project)... I did not know I could do... I feel better for knowing.

Closely related to what young people knew about the Children Act 1989, was what young people knew about their legal status and rights. Almost all the young people had come into care before the Children Act. They knew broadly whether they were being 'looked after' on a voluntary basis or under a care order. They were generally less clear, and in most cases less interested, about what type of order and the implications of that order, but felt they had a right to know. Young people 'of sufficient understanding to make an informed decision' were not always being informed of their right to refuse a medical, psychiatric or other assessment.

25

My legal status? I have been to court... they did not consider my wishes and feelings... they gave me 21 days...!

Legal status: I am certainly not married!

What is the age you can ask the court to change things? When can you leave care?

Ward of court means every time I need a hair cut I have to ask the court. Care order just means I have to ask the social worker!

If they have care and control and a ward of court on you, you are sunk.

I have all my papers at home... I asked for everything to be photocopied and they did.

Everybody has a right to know their legal status.

Medicals... do you have to have them? They thought I was mad basically... taking me to all these medicals.

According to what I have been told, my mother still has full parental rights over me now it is changed to 'being accommodated'...

Religious persuasion, racial origin, cultural and linguistic background

Section 22 of the Children Act specifies that 'due consideration' should be given to the child's religious persuasion, racial origin and cultural and linguistic background. The professional helping relationship with a young person is very far from an equal partnership. But acknowledging, respecting and supporting difference, and challenging discrimination is important in ensuring more equal working relationships.

They tried to make me learn my language... I don't want to learn it... none of my other family speak it... What I am trying to say is that they should have asked me if I wanted it in the first place... I do stick to my culture... I don't eat, I have always done that, my family does that.

They tried to force me to go to the Mosque... come on they said, you are going today. What is the use of taking me when I am just going to walk out. The right to choose is b-t man.

He got into trouble with one of the teachers because he was racist, and he only got into trouble because the teacher was racist (a complaint was made). The teacher had a very bad reprimand.

When you say you are in a children's home people think you are a tramp or something.

26

You say you are in care and lots of people feel sorry for you. I hate that feeling, because it makes you feel really awful.

Fostered? With me I say it is my family... it avoids problems.

Tell them about care... not for their sympathy... but so they can know how we really are.

The importance of choice

Many young people are also at a disadvantage in the decision-making process because they have not had the experience or the opportunity to develop the necessary skills to participate. Guidance and Regulations on the Children Act specifies that all children need to be given information and appropriate explanations so that they are in a position to develop views and make choices.

Young people who took part in this study, felt it was important that they had more opportunities to make real choices in their lives. Not just big choices about where to live, and who to live with, but choices about the day to day running of their establishment, involvement in making up the rules of the establishments, residents meetings etc. Working in partnership with young people is about helping them develop the knowledge and skills to make choices.

I did not want to go to boarding school... don't let them trick you, that's what they did to me.

We did not really have a choice. I was split from my brother and sister.

The only choice I have had is where I would live when I left the children's home.

Life story work... I said no, I did not want to do it... But my brother had to do it. It is not fair. They wrote 'when you were five your mother died.' Then my social worker said she wanted me to see a psychiatrist... to help me get over my grief... I said I had got over it... she said I had not got over it properly...

Choices? Yes I do get choices (choosing food, involvement in residents' meetings etc).

One of the most important decisions young people living away from home have to make, is how much contact they want with their families.

Families

Local authorities have a duty under the Children Act to promote the upbringing of children by their families (Children Act section 17(1)), and to promote contact between the child and his or her parents and other people of significance when they are looking after that child. (Children Act schedule 2 (15)).

Young people in the project welcomed the greater efforts that are to be made under the Children Act 1989 to keep families together. A number of young people were bitter that in the past, they had been removed from their families unnecessarily. The dilemma in the partnership relationship is whose views should rule the day? Those of the parents or those of the young person? The project highlighted the wisdom of listening to the young people. Most young people knew whether or not they wanted contact with their family, and wanted their views respected, even if this might involve an element of risk to them. When their views were not respected, they sometimes found other means of achieving what they wanted.

We should try hard to stick with our families.

For a start I don't think children should be taken away. Like now they try to keep you with your parents as much as possible. We did not have any help at all, we were just whisked away that was it.

You should be allowed to go and see your family unless you are in danger. But if you are not in danger, I think you should he allowed to see your family when you want to. At the moment my social worker is saying no, but I am still going behind her back and going to see them.

At the end of the day everyone has to have contact with their family...

Under the Children Act you are supposed to stay near your parents and family... but if you have been sexually abused (you get moved away).

When they tell ME it is a good idea to see my family, I tell them where to go.

If there is a family they should be put together... in my case... that would have helped us to stick together... now we are separated we are all split up... if they did some rearranging they could keep most of the families together.

There was this girl... a really lonely girl...very timid and shy... they said they couldn't get her a place with her sister. She moved with my foster mother... she played up... then they put her to live with her sister... Now that could have been done all along because there were beds. I asked the social worker and she told me they did it to see how they would act if they were apart. They are children and when they take you away from your Mam at such a young age it does affect you badly... why are social workers doing this?

I have been away for so long I don't want to go home. My Dad used to be battering me every day, and I don't want that anymore... I can't put up with all that.

Many of these decisions should be made at planning meetings and reviews.

Planning meetings and reviews

Local authorities have a duty under the Children Act to conduct regular reviews of children and young people being looked after. They are also advised to provide a system which will ensure the fullest participation of both parents and children in the decision-making process. (DOH, 1991: G&R Vol 4, 3.8).

In this case partnership is about facilitating this participation. However, many young people who took part in the project were not able to participate in their reviews and consequently felt it was a waste of time attending. They also felt intimidated by large meetings. Sometimes they would have preferred not to have certain people there but felt unable to say so. They felt things were better where they had a quiet discussion before their review with their social worker/key worker and where planning meetings and reviews were held at times convenient to families and the young person.

How can I speak...they are talking about my family... I can't talk about what I want with them there.

I have been to one...I did speak but I did not say everything I wanted to say. I couldn't really say it in case I upset my key worker.

When I found out things did not change, I did not bother to go.

It is better to talk to your social worker first, you can tell her what you think.

It is just a waste of time... they are always making the decisions aren't they? They are not speaking to you, they are just telling you what you have to do.

Can I take someone else along to my review?

(At reviews) when you have something to say, they do not give you enough time to get it out.

If you had a choice of where to have the review/planning meeting, I think it would be better out in the community away from the children's home.

They say they will let you know and then they don't, not until the next review.

Aftercare

Partnership is also about preparing young people for when they become independent, and supporting them if they need it after they have left care. Section 24 of the Children Act says that the local authority have a duty to advise, assist and befriend young people when they cease to be looked after. Young people who took part in the project, especially those soon to leave care, were very anxious about their futures. They did not feel they had the necessary preparation. They did not know what their rights were.

Aftercare... I don't want to think about it.

Aftercare... is that like 'afterlife'... reincarnation!

At home I started cooking at nine. When I was in care I did not start until I was 13.

Can I change a plug? ... we are not allowed to do any of that at the home. We get an electrician in.

Social services... they can't just leave me because I would get into a lot of trouble.

Money is the biggest problem on leaving care.

I visited my old home (residential establishment) and it was quite painful when I was told to go away. No-one told me that I would have nothing. I can't afford to eat, let alone pay for train fares (to visit DSS office). That's why I want to join the army.

I think I am ready to be out of care... but it makes you frightened... even though social services are a load of c-p there is security that there is always somebody there. They said I was capable... and although I've been in care nine years, they can't just put me out.

Money was important not only for those leaving care, it was important to all young people.

Allowances

Although money is, for most of us, central to our lives, it is strange how often the importance of this is overlooked when working with young people in care. Money, and knowing how much you can expect, is power. Money matters, in one way or another, generated more discussion in this project than anything else. Young people needed to know about their likely allowances in order to make choices in their day to day lives, and to plan their future. Young people were severely disempowered by the arbitrary way many decisions relating to pocket money and other allowances appeared to be made. The partnership issue here, is being open and fair about money matters.

You need to know about money.

They don't tell you about pocket money.

We all get the same... no matter what age you are.

We spend most of our pocket money on hair things and the like...

I went to Germany and I got some money...

You can apply for money... but don't always get it. Aunt and Uncle get a small allowance for me... things like trips and a new bike... that is not out of the money they are given...

Can you get a grant if you go to college?

I have to have some special paper for Braille... do I have to pay for this out of my money? I have to pay £1.35 for the paper... for homework and for general writing... I like writing stories...

Some kids get more than others. I was a bit spoilt because I helped.

If you don't ask you don't get it. They don't tell you what you are entitled to... they are just saving money.

It ought to be written down the money you're entitled to.

It would be fairer if there were set allowances... but some kids have special needs.

An accessible and independent complaints procedure is one way of airing these views.

Problems/complaints

An essential criteria in the partnership relationship is the facility to make a complaint if the young person feels this is necessary. Section

26(3) of the Children Act 1989, requires the responsible authority to establish a procedure for considering any complaint made to them by any child who is being looked after by them, or who is not being looked after by them but is in need. In this study, the complaints procedure was better known than most parts of the Children Act 1989. Most young people had heard about it and some had made use of it to good advantage. This seemed to be where they were supported in making their complaint. Others did not bother because they felt they could not get the help they needed, or as it was part of social services, they thought they would not get anywhere.

> *I knew that it wasn't right, but I didn't know what it was, and I didn't know what to do about it.*

> *Everybody should know about the complaints procedure.*

> *Complaints procedure? They are not around... I had to ask. You have to ask for them... They don't have them on display.*

> *People who live independently (age 16 plus) aren't told about the complaints procedure. I haven't been told anything.*

> *When you complain, they are supposed to come back and tell you.*

> *I made a complaint once, but I don't know what happened to it. Complaints procedure? I don't need it!*

Relationships

This was not one of the original topics for discussion but was brought up by young people in all the groups. Meaningful relationships give purpose to life. Many young people who have been in care and who may have moved around from placement to placement, may not have had the opportunity to make and keep friends. The Children Act Guidance and Regulations notes that the capacity to form satisfying relationships and achieve interdependence with others is crucial to the future well-being of the young person. Working with young people is therefore about helping them to form other relationships and other partnerships. The professional partnership should not be exclusive.

> *I find it hard to explain, but because I have been brought up in children's homes I find it really hard to form relationships. It is probably because I have been brought up in care, and have kept moving around.*

> *I have nothing in common with anyone who has not been in care... I am 17 going on 40... how can you sit there and talk about cars all night... the biggest problem they have had is how to get the newest BMW.*

32

An important issue was the concern young people expressed about their education.

Education issues

Children who have been looked after by local authorities often need extra help and encouragement, and opportunities to compensate for early deprivation and for educational disadvantage. Local authorities are specifically reminded that in looking after young people, they should have regard to the importance of continuity of education and that they should provide educational opportunities and support (DOH, 1991: G&R Vol 4)

However, up to a third of young people who took part in the Dolphin Project were out of school/further education/work training. The number of children in residential care who are out of school overall may be even higher. In each area, education was raised by young people as a matter of concern. In all areas there were young people 'being looked after' who were missing out on schooling, not getting sufficient help in returning to school, and some young people were not getting the necessary peace and quiet to do homework. Many of the young people we spoke to, wanted much more support and help in their education. In some residential establishments being out of school was the 'norm' rather than the exception.

In the partnership relationship, the young person is who is in care needs a powerful advocate to ensure that the child has equality of opportunity, and that means equality of access to education.

I have missed loads and loads of schooling. I want home tutoring.

I'm not at school at the moment... I don't fit into normal comprehensive... there is no help or encouragement to go back to school.

No-one listens when I tell them I am bullied.

I passed into grammar school... I misbehaved (and was suspended) it was all this moving about (in care).

I went back to the fifth year again because I moved around in care. I have been out of school for four months.

There is no quiet room at X... If you want to be quiet you have to go to the toilet.

I get no help with any form of homework.

I wish I had stayed at the same school because every children's home I went to I changed school. One day I woke up and thought I am not getting anywhere. The teacher said you are a 'no hoper', you will leave school with nothing... but... (he is now at college).

Bullying

Partnership is about protecting young people from significant harm and supporting them through tough patches. Local authorities have a duty under the Children Act to safeguard and promote the welfare of those they are looking after (Children Act 1989 section 22(3). However, the level of bullying in residential establishments mentioned by some young people in the project, and the apparent inability of the staff to contain this, fell far short of the principles of the legislation.

> *I am not being disgusting, but the kids run riot in XX home.*

> *When we were getting bullied, my Dad said something to the head. That home had a reputation for that... it is closed down now.*

> *There is so... much aggro in there and the kids were really horrible.*

> *I was at this children's home. The kids used to pick on my brother... I used to stick up for my brother and then I would get the shit kicked out of me... we complained but they did not do anything.*

> *You really do have to stick up for yourselves in some children's homes... you really do.*

> *My brother was lying there and someone else was punching him bad... and a member of staff standing there doing nothing. I said... you should be sorting this out... she said I am not going to get hurt and I had to threaten her so she would help my brother.*

> *I've had a really hard time... I've been picked on and bullied... If you tell the social workers you are known as a grasser and get even more...*

> *I have seen him coming down in the morning crying... it is so bad... now like today... he did not want to eat...he did not want to work... he is not usually like that.*

A major concern was that in some cases bullying leads to more serious repercussions. In one area up to a third of the young people who took part in the project spontaneously stated that they had undertaken acts with the intention of ending their lives. When young people were in distress, the role of the professional carer is crucial.

Carers

The best partner for the young person being looked after was often their key worker. Young people knew what they wanted from their carers. Surprisingly, front line residential and foster carers received a better press from the young people than field social workers.

Some of them are good... some of them are wasting their time being there. They walk about cleaning the kitchen and setting the tables. It is nice when all the kids and all the staff get together and have discussions.

They have got to discipline you... but they do it the wrong way. You have to respect the carers and they have to respect us.

Staff need personal qualities and staff need training.

I think a good carer is someone who sits down and listens to you... and someone who will follow it through for you and try to sort the problem out.

They go to college but that won't give them experience.

Social workers... they sit in the office... moving all the kids around...people who actually work in children's home and do all the dirty work. I think they understand.

Summary: Criteria for working in partnership with young people who are being looked after

This research suggests that young people are very keen to work in partnership with those making decisions about their lives and this partnership is very productive. Where the problem arises, is with those making the decisions. The Children Act calls for a major shift in values and attitudes and central to this shift is partnership principle. Working in partnership with families is one leap forward, but working in partnership with children is another gigantic leap. Imposing decisions on young people is, in the short term, considerably easier than facilitating the negotiating process. In this study many carers felt they needed more training for this task. The study also suggested that sometimes the decision-making was too far removed from the young people and that it may be better if more power was delegated to their immediate carers, especially to make the day to day decisions that affect a young person's life.

The following summarizes the key findings. The professional partner should be willing and able to:
- share information with that young person about his or her rights under the law and make sure that the young person fully understands the implication of any legal order affecting him/her
- acknowledge difference whether due to racial origin, language, religion, culture or disability; respect and support young people and challenge discrimination
- make opportunities for young people to make choices and to learn about making decisions

35

- remember that in dealing with parents, young people are also partners in the decision-making and may need support in making their views known
- help young people to participate in their reviews
- prepare young people for independence
- share information about pocket money and allowances
- support young people in making a complaint
- help young people develop other relationships, other partnerships
- advocate for young people in obtaining equal opportunity in education
- recognize and support young people in distress
- recognize that the best professional partner may be the key residential or foster carer.

4 Partnership and the Children Act 1989

THE LOCAL AUTHORITY'S POWERS AND DUTIES

Rob Hutchinson

The context

The Children Act seeks to change attitudes. Change can be a current buzz word, but it is important to be clear about what needs to be changed and why, so that change is not undertaken for change's sake. Twenty-one years ago generic social services departments were born. At that time certain attitudes prevailed. First and foremost was the influence of the Children and Young Persons Act 1969, which in turn was heavily influenced by a White Paper drawn up on the 1960's, The Child, the Family and the Young Offender (DHSS, 1966) This White Paper was based on a psycho-analytic approach and suggested for every problem there was an underlying insecurity to be sorted out. State care was seen as a solution to children and young people's problems. A spell in an approved school or long-term foster care provided answers to the non-coping parent. Trained social workers were scarce but the expectations from professional intervention were high. Not only had social workers the skills to understand clients' problems, often in a way which clients did not themselves realize, but they also had at their disposal, during the 1970s expanding budgets and many resources.

The first of the public child abuse tragedies, Maria Colwell, identified the need for multi-agency cooperation in child protection. It also confirmed the correctness of the need to take very strong action to protect children against parents who were not up to the task. The professional was in charge and was drawing up the policies.

At the start of the 1980s this all started to change, largely because of the squeeze on public expenditure, and because managers took over from the professionals in the need to reduce expensive forms of service and resources. Young people were brought back, or not sent to expensive out-of-county Community Homes, and children's homes were closed. The managers and politicians were driving the policies, and in Hampshire this led to our Child Care Strategy towards the end of the 1980's, where the revenue from closed children's homes was re-invested in Community Services designed to keep families together. Also, as a result of a re-evaluation of the attitudes about care being a solution rather than in many cases the cause of problems, a major shift was made in the way in which decisions about children's lives were taken, which in turn lead to more child/parental involvement in our formal/informal processes like case conferences.

Meanwhile, in the outside world the market place was becoming a more competitive place and consumers were becoming King and Queen. Consumer research, consumer information, quality standards and requests for feedback on services are now to be found everywhere, and the culture and requirement now exists for consumer involvement and empowerment. This is what will make the 1990s the opportunity and the challenge for all concerned to achieve services which meet the needs of individuals and groups of individuals. Whether we use jargon such as 'Care Management' or simply say we have to get people what they need, the message is clear for the large organizations, things have to change.

The vision

So what does the Children Act say about partnership, what is the expectation by consumers of what it means and what is the long-term vision?

Principles of the Children Act 1989
- The child's welfare is paramount
- Children should be brought up by their families
- Services for children 'in need'
- Partnership with children, parents and other agencies
- Child protection but open to challenge
- The child's voice
- Continuing role of parents and the wider family
(Hampshire Social Services)

The first principle is the paramountcy of the child's welfare, but all the others emphasize the parental and family context. Of particular interest is the guidance about services for children in need.

38

Services for children 'in need'

Help should:
- be provided in partnership with the parents
- meet each child's identified needs
- be appropriate in terms of the child's race, culture, religion and linguistic background
- be open to effective, independent representations and complaints procedures
- draw upon effective collaboration between different agencies, including those in the voluntary sector

(Hampshire Social Services)

These principles highlight the role of parents. In *Children Act 1989 Guidance and Regulations for Children with Disabilities* (DOH, 1991: G&R Vol 6) parents are referred to as experts, but how many parents of children in need are in fact encouraged to see themselves as having some expertise in this role? These principles also stress that services must meet children's needs not the other way round, and that we have to be sensitive to cultural and racial needs. In Hampshire this is something which in the main we are not good at. Effective collaboration between agencies is emphasized as another principle, and this refers to both sharing resources for the individual's needs, as well as when collaborating for planning purposes.

Partnership from the local authority's point of view has different dimensions. It means listening; it means giving up power and control; it means sharing influence in relation to big issues like the development of new services such as Child Development Centres or Child Protection Services or participation in decisions about individual children. My own view is we should aim to to create a sense of 'one community'. I am haunted by the idea of the person who comes down to earth from Mars and sees a disjointed, unco-ordinated range of services controlled by different organizations with different objectives, many of whom have personal power objectives forcing them apart. The challenge of the Children Act, and indeed the consumers' objective, is to bring organizations together, to gain a common view of the needs of children and family for the future, to share resources and to think in terms of a jigsaw, some with large pieces, some with small, but all important. I constantly emphasize that Social Services provides .001% of all the help and support in the world: the rest is provided by friends, relations, communities, and those are the resources that we must locate, tell people about and build upon. Assumptions should not be made that more services are automatically going to Social Services Departments, Health Authorities or large organizations. In many cases it is the small voluntary organizations that must be built on.

Key areas and issues

We need to be clear what we mean by partnership, who are the potential parties and what we need to do to create the partnership. One thing is certain, we mean different things depending on what we do, whether we are a child in need or a parent, whether we work in Social Services, the Health Authority or a voluntary organization. Different perspectives will give different measurements of partnership. The Black communities will want to know whether we understand the perspectives and needs of black consumers, whether we have black staff who can assess those needs and wants in a credible way and whether our services are sensitive to those needs and wants. Children with disabilities and their families want information, equal access to services as other children, and an equal say in where their children are educated. Partnership means a shared responsibility in all decisions, whether they are individual plans or services on a large scale, and this can create conflict. What happens to advocacy if voluntary organizations are on the inside of the planning process and become reasonable and understanding instead of pushing and demanding? These are all ideals, but what is the reality? Where are the problems, what is stopping us achieving these things and where are the achievements?

Achievements

The need to change attitudes was mentioned earlier. One of the key changes that society has to acknowledge is that generally the state does not make a good parent. In December 1987 there were 2212 children in care in Hampshire. Five years on Hampshire 'looked after' 1115 children. Demographic changes have played a part, but only a comparatively small one, a far greater influence has been commitment to finding the least intrusive way of supporting children in need and to minimize the authority that Social Services can wield. Working with children and parents with agreement rather than using force, through Care Orders and Emergency Protection Orders or Place of Safety Orders, increases co-operation as well as the likelihood of keeping families together or returning children to their families. There is plenty of research to demonstrate this, but Jean Packman's work in Hampshire (Packman et al., 1986) and Jane Rowe's outcomes in child care (Rowe et al., 1984, 1989) are important examples.

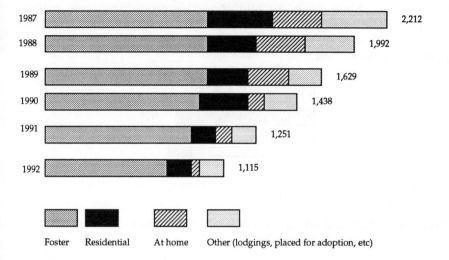

Figure 4.1 Number of children looked after in Hampshire 1987-1992

The following figure demonstrates the dramatic change in this period in the use of Protection Orders.

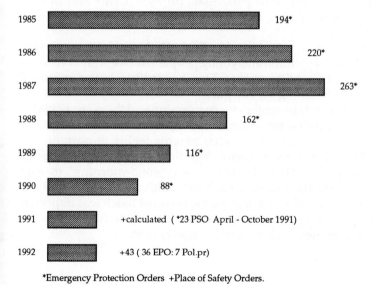

*Emergency Protection Orders +Place of Safety Orders.

Figure 4.2 Number of Place of Safety/Emergency Protection Orders in Hampshire 1985-1992

Another measurement is the involvement of parents in Child protection Conferences. When the 1981 Child protection procedures were written it was explicitly stated that parents would be excluded. Since May 1990 that policy has been reversed and percentages of attendances in the periods are illustrated.

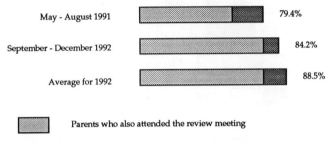

May - August 1991   79.4%

September - December 1992   84.2%

Average for 1992   88.5%

Parents who also attended the review meeting

Figure 4.3   Parental attendance at Child Protection Conferences in Hampshire 1991-1992

As far as children's reviews are concerned, the average figure for attendances by children is eighty percent. This is not bad, but of course it is what happens in the review or, more particularly, whether the child or young person thinks that he or she can influence the plans for his/her life or the way that he/she is being looked after, that are the real issues. Adults tend to invite to participate on their terms and in their world, and I have no doubt that we still have much to learn about listening to children.

Recently Hampshire launched a 'Listening to Children' initiative, which sought out the views of children and young people who we were consulting in a series of 'child friendly' events. This has lead to better informed practice and better listening on our part.

There are other possible indicators for partnership and these are available. However, I am aware that these are drawn up from the Social Services perspective and it may not reflect what parents feel is important. The Westminster Bank decided some while ago they were going to be more user-friendly and instructed all staff to say 'good-morning' to each client, smile and use their name. They then did a survey to find out what the customer wanted and, although the personal touch was important it rated about twentieth on the list. What was most important was knowing that the money in their account was correct.

Barriers

There are of course limits to individual partnership, if by partnership one means equal and shared responsibility between the various people involved. For example, there are some situations where the child's welfare means that partnership cannot operate because the parents have done the child significant harm. There may be cases where the child' s interests or wishes conflict with the parents', but these situations should be, and are, comparatively few. More likely barriers are lack of understanding between potential partners because of lack of clarity; a failure to listen and hear, and the inappropriate use of jargon. However, the major factor is the willingness to acknowledge that the power relationship is totally out of balance in terms of reality and perception. Stereotypes exist for all of us, whether we are visiting the doctor, meeting a senior manager or, more particularly, what power we know someone else has should they wish to exercize it. The power to remove a child, the power to refuse help or resources when someone is in a crisis, or simply the realization that there is something happening to you over which other people have control, are the most intimidating of situations. Sometimes the reality may be that the child is in danger and power has to be exercized, but the more the parent is involved in what is happening and why, the greater the chance of achieving cooperation, understanding and, if necessary, a change in behaviour. There are responsibilities which mean that the final say will be with the Family Proceedings Court, the Social Services Department or, say, the Police, but so long as the parameters are explicit then collaboration and co-operation can still exist. Many of the problems lie in misunderstandings and perceptions of secrecy by key people. Genuine openness and honesty will go some way to overcoming the barriers. However, the responsibility remains for ensuring the welfare of the child and this has to be the primary objective. Staff should not in any way feel compromised into believing otherwise. There is a danger here, in child protection terms, that partnership and a good relationship with parents could become more important than an objective assessment of the needs of the child. I would always defend social workers because the vast majority do a difficult job in an outstanding way. However, the pressure of the mass media sitting on their shoulders in case they make a mistake, must not stand in the way of realizing we have to continue to change and improve.

Planning

I would like to say a word about planning services for children and families. The Children Act draws attention to the need to involve other organizations in planning services. If one takes a symbolic view of wanting to put together a jigsaw puzzle, everyone who is relevant needs to be involved in the particular planning group. Partnership here is complicated, and getting everyone involved has time and money constraints, different and sometimes conflicting organizational objectives and unreal expectations. There are problems for the large organizations in giving up some of the power that their resources bring, and difficulties for some consumer organizations who have to learn that money is finite and that often it runs out. However, the only realistic way of moving forward is to accept that if we are to meet the needs of children in need, whether they are in crisis or experiencing deprivation of play facilities or proper housing, we have to recognize that we have to pool ideas and resources and not stick to our own narrow responsibilities. The perspective of sharing problems, as well as resources, is obvious and there are lots of good examples everywhere. However, we have a long way to go.

The situation of young homeless people could surely be improved with more imagination, support of young families could be better coordinated and, above all, the sharing of information could be organized in a way that is easily accessible to those who want that information. Young homeless people have particular needs, though organizations in planning terms tend to focus on the obvious ones such as accommodation or benefits. It makes sense for Housing, Social Services and Social Security to plan services with young people, though I suspect they do not often get invited, nor asked about what they would like. The health needs of homeless young people are sometimes overlooked. Psychiatric disorders such as depression, contraceptive advice or free contraception, dental requirements often brought on by poor nutrition, all put Health Authorities into the jigsaw with important services to contribute. Employment opportunities, whilst not that numerous for anyone, need particular attention, and careers and employers federations such as Chambers of Commerce must be pulled into discussions. The involvement of the private sector should not be lost sight of, there is a community responsibility for all parts of the community. The Church in its broadest form has a long standing record for helping homeless people, as do a wide variety of voluntary organizations including housing associations. The need for information and publicity about what is available for homeless young people suggests that local radio, as well as the local evening papers, can be asked to play their part in getting information through to the young people. However, all these things rather beg the question of what do the young people want. The Regional Health Authority and Social Services are engaged in some research to go out and ask them what is needed, and if it is possible to meet their requirements the aim must be to try and get them to feel they have some power to influence and drive the changes. Few groups can feel as dependent or powerless.

The future

As far as the future is concerned; partnership with individuals will have to increase, large organizations and staff will have to listen to what people say they need, and we will all have to work harder at making this easier for our clients. In the Health Service, an artificial split between purchasers and providers has been created, largely to ensure that patients are able to get what they need rather than more of the same services which continue almost with a life of their own. Community Care is demanding a care management approach where individual staff ensure a needs led approach. I believe the Children Act demands a similar approach and the Hampshire Child Care Strategy is a fair way along that path, but not far enough. Part of the reason is to do with resources, and partly to do with the need for an increasingly flexible approach. On the planning side, we need representative groups of organizations and users to jointly develop services and to ensure that individual organizations do not go off on their own without involving others. Some of these systems exist but most are incomplete. In some areas enormous amounts of energy and time have been consumed in setting up consumer groups and joint groups with statutory and voluntary organizations. It has complicated what was formerly a simple autocratic system but it has begun to create common aims and trust.

If I was to evaluate how Hampshire are doing in relation to where we have come from I would say we are doing reasonably well. If I had to assess Hampshire in terms of where we have got to go I would say we have a long, long way to go but at least we are on the move. To progress we must all see ourselves as just a part of the jigsaw and we must listen.

Part Three
RECENT RESEARCH AND SPECIALIST PRACTICE

5 Partnership with black and minority ethnic communities

SERVICES FOR CHILDREN UNDER EIGHT

Nina Swarup and Carol Hayden

Workshop discussion reported by Kish Bhatti-Sinclair

Background

> Children from a very young age learn about different races and
> cultures including religion and languages and will be capable of
> assigning different values to them.
>
> (DOH, 1991: G&R Vol 2, p34)

There is a wide range of services for young children which may have a
significant impact on the values and behaviour of the next generation.
These facilities include; family support services, for example family
centres and family resource centres, child guidance clinics, day care;
education provision; as well as a whole range of supervised activities,
such as playgroups, creche facilities, clubs and leisure activities. The
Children Act gives a new impetus to debates about how best to encourage
positive attitudes to different races and cultures, as well as how to
improve involvement and participation rates of black and minority
ethnic groups in some of these services.

Lane (1989) writing for the Commission for Racial Equality, describes
the Children Act as a positive step forward for providing children's day
care and education services, because the Act is founded on principles of
equality of opportunity and anti-discriminatory practice. However, Lane
in common with other commentators on the Act, raises some major
concerns about how this will translate into practice, for example: how
race and cultural issues are incorporated into the registration, inspection

49

and review responsibilities; the availability of appropriate skills to support and train staff; the availability of resources to ensure implementation of these aspects of the Act. Other commentators, such as Stubbs (1991), whilst applauding the fact that the Act represents some progress, are critical that it does not recognize racism in terms of power and oppression but simply reflects an emphasis on 'difference'.

This chapter will describe the findings from two pieces of research at the Social Services Research and Information Unit at the University of Portsmouth, as well as include the discussions and information provided at a workshop, which formed part of the Partnership in Practice Conference at Southampton University in 1992. The focus in research terms is specifically on the requirements of the Act in relation to day care and supervised activities for under-eights and how this relates to possibilities for fostering partnership between services and black and minority ethnic communities. However, many of the issues about partnership are of course general and do not necessarily relate only to under-eights services.

Requirements of the Children Act

There are a number of clear requirements for local authorities to encourage positive developments with black and minority ethnic communities:

- **provision of day care**
  local authorities are 'to have regard to the different racial groups to which children within their area who are 'in need' belong';

- **registration of facilities**
  local authorities have the power to cancel the registration of a facility, where the facility is making inadequate recognition of children's religious persuasion, racial origin and cultural and linguistic background;

- **approved equal opportunities policies**
  local authorities should have approved equal opportunities policies, including arrangements for monitoring and reviewing progress towards implementation;

- **assessments on service provision for black and minority ethnic groups**
  local authorities have to ensure that they have available data on the ethnic origins of the local population, in order to assess the extent to which local services are operating in a non-discriminatory way;

- **service review**
  services for young children were the subject of a review

during the first year of implementation of the Act and thereafter every three years. Local authorities have a duty to ensure that all racial groups within the area contribute fully. This may involve providing interpreter and translation services, as well as seeing that arrangements for consultative meetings and their membership do not discriminate
(DOH, 1991, G&R Vol 2 p34).

Partnership with black and minority ethnic communities

The Children Act (1989) places emphasis on partnership with the children's families so as to make better provision for the children's needs. The Act requires that parents and children be consulted during the decision-making process and be notified of the outcome.

Evidence from Swarup (1992) shows that, as yet, very little consultation has taken place between service providers and black communities. Some black parents in this study expressed concern regarding the well-being of their children, but felt they did not have sufficient knowledge of the education system nor of other service provision to be able to influence decisions which may affect their children.

The lack of appropriate service provision in terms of the needs of children and families from black and minority ethnic communities was a major finding of the report. Black people felt that their religious, cultural and language needs were often not taken into account. They were therefore not receiving the same quality of service as the rest of the population. Several people said they would not use some services as they did not cater for their needs, for example, an Iranian girl said in relation to social services:

> ... *if* I had a problem, I don't really think I would go to them (social services). I would want to tell someone who I feel would understand, someone who understands my culture.
> (Swarup, 1992, p.62)

Although the Children Act begins to address the issue of identifying the needs of black children and families, the information is vague and limited. It has also been criticized for not addressing the issue of racism.

In Swarup's study, service providers interviewed felt that the lack of contact and consultation with black families was due to language difficulties. Yet the survey shows that just over half (52%) of all respondents were fluent in English. Therefore, language should not remain a barrier, service providers can contact those who do speak English and also provide interpreters for those who are not fluent in English.

Existing mechanisms to consult local communities' views have often neglected the views of black people. Ways to encourage black people to participate need to be found if equality of opportunity is to be achieved. Several black groups suggested that the venue and time of consultative groups need to be reviewed if they are to include black people. Meetings held in places of authority were viewed as intimidating. Black people reported that they were more likely to attend meetings held in the local community. In relation to the times of meetings it may be that the conventional 'nine to five' day does not fit into the lifestyle of some communities. Early evenings and weekends and/or more flexible attitudes to meeting times should be considered.

The misconception that contacting the so-called 'community leaders' will represent the views of the whole community still exists among many local authorities. Most 'community leaders' are men and may therefore not represent the views of women. The need for more information about the services available and the opportunities for consultation to be distributed in the local communities was felt to be important. It was stressed that this information should be jargon-free and written in clear, simple English to be translated into different languages if necessary. Also, it was felt that out-reach work is initially needed to build confidence and encourage people to participate in meetings.

Existing consultative groups were seen as too formal and rigid, where consultation was often not a matter of getting the views of the communities but rather a means of telling the groups what was going to be done regardless of their views. Many black people reported that they were tired of consultation which was merely 'talk' without the power to act on their decisions.

A real commitment to the ideals of partnership and participation would necessitate some degree of power-sharing so that black communities could have an influence in the decision-making process.

Services for young children (under eights)

This section reports on the first stage of an ongoing research project (Hayden, 1992) on the Children Act which has been commissioned by Hampshire Social Services Department.

Parts of the research project looked at the registration process for day care and supervised activities for children under eight years, as well as the equal opportunities consciousness of Hampshire social service staff. A summary of the findings in these two areas follows.

The registration process

Hampshire's fifty day care officers are charged with the registration and inspection of services for under-eights by the Children Act. In the first year of implementation (1991-1992) this involved only pre-school services, but has subsequently included the five to eight year old group. Registering services for pre-school children alone is a massive undertaking, with an estimated 4,412 childminders, 842 playgroups as well as the other less numerous facilities such as nurseries and creches. What follows is some feedback from this process as it relates to issues about race and ethnicity and anti-discriminatory practice.

Information about participation rates of children from black and minority ethnic groups in day care and supervised activities for under-eights, is not as yet available on an organized basis. The perception is that such children are conspicuous by their absence in many facilities, and it can be difficult to move beyond this impasse with some service providers when they are registered by day care officers from social services. Part of Hampshire's registration process involves service providers signing an anti-discrimination statement. However, this is only the beginning in what is clearly a much longer process, as these quotes from day care officers illustrate:

> *The problem isn't with the statement. It's more about 'what is multicultural play?' and 'is it important?'... The reaction of people so far is... 'I haven't had any children of other races'... they think that if their children are not mixing with children of other races that they don't need to think about it...*

> *Most providers think it's about treating people the same, they don't understand about acknowledging difference.*

Although day care officers have had training for the registration process, including training on race awareness, this still led to the feeling on the part of some officers that:

> *It's difficult to challenge on race. I don't feel I know enough to respond to the challenge.*

Clearly, good quality on-going training opportunities incorporating anti-discriminatory and anti-racist practice are essential. It is a first step in ensuring that those involved in providing, as well as registering, inspecting and reviewing services for young children, are supported in reaching the standards required by the Children Act, as the Guidance and Regulations to this part of the Act advises:

> People working with young children should value and respect the different racial origins, religions, cultures and languages in a multi-racial society so that each child is valued as an individual without racial or gender stereotyping.
>
> (DOH, 1991: G&R Vol 2)

Equal opportunities consciousness

The provision of equal opportunities for children underpins the Children Act in a number of ways. The requirement to identify and provide services for children 'in need' is arguably part of this. However, as already indicated, attention to issues of 'race and culture' are very explicitly part of the provisions of the Children Act.

All representatives of the seventeen area social services centres in Hampshire were very conscious of equal opportunities issues. In fact the first equal opportunities issue to come to mind in fifteen of the areas was that of race and ethnicity. This was perhaps not surprising given the recent implementation of a race policy for Hampshire Social Services. There was a tendency amongst staff to feel that training on race and ethnicity should be part of a broader equal opportunities approach, rather than specifically about race and ethnicity, as the following quotes illustrate:

> *Equal opportunities issues underpinned all the Children Act training .... We are weaker on class and culture, religion and gender than on race and ethnicity... yet the majority of our users are working class people, it's not even on the County agenda.*

> *All the managers have had the race training, rather than anti-discriminatory training which I think is a pity ... I think it should have been broader... the training should be transferable.*

However, in relation to getting appropriate advice and help on race outside social services, there was a tendency to focus on just two facilities; the Community Liaison Unit in Portsmouth, and Southampton Council for Community Service. In many parts of the County these facilities were some distance away which led to a reliance on social services staff, leading to a feeling that:

> *We can use people inappropriately... it's everybody's responsibility.*

Workshop discussion

Workshop discussion focused on three main issues about partnership with black and minority ethnic communities and the requirements of the Children Act. These were:
- **contact** with and **participation** of black and minority ethnic communities in relation to under-eights services;
- **training** for staff managing and delivering these services;
- the possibilities for **power sharing** as part of the process of developing consultation and participation in services.

The range of services for children under eight years is very broad, but offers a number of possibilities in terms of contact with, and the participation of black and minority ethnic communities. By law all children have to have some form of organized education at the age of five years, which for most children takes place in a school environment. This provides a potential avenue of opportunity for children from different racial and cultural groups to mix freely, as well as the possibility of a wider involvement of parents from all racial and ethnic groups.

However, with pre-school children, patterns of access are more complex. Some evidence suggests that children from some ethnic groups may not participate in pre-school activities to the same extent as their white peers. Whether this is so in Hampshire, or indeed elsewhere, is not as yet routinely monitored. Clearly monitoring participation in all pre-school facilities is a necessary pre-requisite for action to improve such participation.

Swarup's work (Swarup, 1992) has already identified a general lack of consultation with black and minority ethnic groups on the part of some service providers in the fields of health, housing and social services, although this is a requirement under the Children Act. Participants in the workshop also highlighted that such consultation was in its infancy. Furthermore, participation rates of children from black and minority ethnic communities in services, other than education, were perceived to be low.

Concern focused on who to consult and how to consult, as the first step towards improving participation rates of black and minority ethnic children in under-eights services. The tendency, highlighted in Swarup's work, was to presume that 'community leaders' could speak for a particular group of people who had race or ethnicity in common. This practice was thought questionable by some workshop participants as such individuals were usually older men, thus the varied nature of a particular group could not be represented. This was true most dramatically with the needs of women, but also with the needs of different age groups as well as the needs of people who had taken on a wide range of other modes of adaptation to life in a predominantly 'white' society.

Staff training

There is an acknowledged nervousness, some participants spoke of 'fear', on the part of many service providers about 'getting things wrong' when it comes to addressing issues of race and ethnicity. This nervousness can translate into a feeling amongst some service providers that they need to arrive at a state of almost total knowledge about race and ethnicity, before they act. However, such a state was also recognized as impossible to achieve and perhaps misses the point. That is, that race and ethnicity is an aspect of an individual's life, not the total means of understanding that individual.

A particular issue of concern in relation to staff training, and of importance to the consultation process is language and the perception that it may be a major barrier in making contact with black and minority ethnic communities. However, as one participant pointed out the majority of people in Britain are second or third generation residents, therefore there are relatively few pockets of people where language forms a major barrier for all members of a family (Swarup, 1992). Nevertheless, interpretation and translation facilities will still be needed, for example it may be inappropriate to use a member of a family to translate for another member about particularly sensitive or personal issues. Furthermore, members of a family may not always be available to act as translators because of employment and other commitments.

Power sharing

Power sharing was described as involving a shift of power from the professional to the service user, or from the organization to the community. In reaching out to black and minority ethnic communities, service providers need to address the issue of the extent to which they are willing to share their power, if at all. If as a result of involving black and minority ethnic service users and communities there are requests for more participation in service planning and the decision-making process, which in turn may result in some changes and adaptations to services, service providers need to be really willing to negotiate this.

Progress and priorities for action: feedback from agencies participating in the workshop

Nine different agencies were represented by twelve individuals. These representatives supplied information about the current state of service provision, training and consultation in relation to black and minority ethnic communities in their agencies. Representatives were also asked about what kinds of action they would prioritize in their organizations. Agencies included: three social services departments (Surrey, Hampshire, Hertfordshire); educational institutions (Open University, University of Portsmouth); and some agencies from the voluntary sector (SCOPE – parents support, Barnardos, Stonham Housing Association, Southampton Council for Community Service).

Current provision

All participants could cite examples of some recognition of the needs of black and minority ethnic groups in their provision of services. Policies were specifically mentioned by half of the participants as a key part of current provision. Two agencies cited a drive to recruit personnel from black and minority ethnic groups and the use of Section 11 funding was mentioned by three agencies. A representative from the Open University cited testing learning materials with different cultural groups as one of the provisions of the OU to recognize the different learning requirements which may arise out of cultural diversity. Materials for children either in waiting rooms or as part of a facilities' service were frequently cited. However, as one representative from a voluntary organization said:

> ... more care needs to go into the selection of resources to make them culturally relevant.

Current training

Training was provided in all but one of the organizations represented in the workshop. Participants were fairly evenly divided between organizations which provided anti-racist and anti-discriminatory training and those which included race and ethnicity as part of a broader equal opportunities framework. Several participants mentioned having outside speakers or consultants on race. One participant commented:

> We've had some anti-racist training, not very successfully carried out, according to my own experience. We used outside white consultants... the training is blurred, I think, by the equal opportunity approach.

Consultation

There was a wide variety of responses and interpretations about what consultation with black and minority ethnic communities might mean. Thus, whilst half the participants reported consultation with black and minority ethnic communities, this could be through a particular facility such as the Community Liaison Unit in Portsmouth and via research projects, or with individual families coming forward to organizations for help. Other participants interpreted consultation in the light of consultation with black workers groups or Asian women's groups, where they exist. Two organizations reported no consultation had taken place from their organizations, whilst another three said very little was happening and/or contact/consultation was 'developing'. One organization reported simply that: 'We work in partnership with all families.'

Participants put forward a range of ideas about action needed. The most frequently expressed need for action (half of the group) was for stronger policies with complaints procedures in place. The availability of information, training and educational materials was mentioned by four participants. More consultation with communities was mentioned by two participants, as was the employment of more black workers.

One participant suggested taking stronger action to recruit black families to services, by approaching health visitors and social workers and getting them to recommend such families, actively.

Conclusions

Evidence from ongoing research (Hayden, 1992; 1993) as well as follow-up consultation on projects like Equal Voice (1992), would indicate that there is a desire and willingness on the part of a wide range of statutory and voluntary agencies, to involve black and minority ethnic families in their services. However, as the responses from many of the agencies participating in this workshop show, the processes of consultation need further development and more training of agency staff is also needed. These are pre-requisites for the development of effective mechanisms for involving families in the process of building a relationship based on partnership between providers of services and black and minority ethnic communities.

The possibilities for building such relationships might be more apparent in the field of children's services, in that children can often act as a bridge between adults in whatever role: parent and parent; parent and professional. Furthermore, the development of working in partnership in the context of working with families with young children, may act as a gateway to other parts of these communities through networks of relatives, friends and neighbours.

The importance of the requirements of the Children Act, in relation to contact with and participation of black and minority ethnic families in services for children under eight years, should not be underestimated. These requirements could be seen as a starting point for creating a more democratic and tolerant society. This is aptly summarized in the following quote from the Commission for Racial Equality (1991):

> We know from research evidence that by the time they enter primary school, white children may be well on the road to believing they are superior to black people. Black children may believe that society is not going to show them the same respect and esteem that white people receive. Such attitudes are not innate, but learned. What is learned before the age of five about

race and race relations is therefore of critical importance to the stability of the next generation and to society as a whole.

(CRE: p22)

6 Recent research

This chapter outlines two recent research studies. The paper by Jackie Powell and Elizabeth Marks of the University of Southampton brings us to the heart of partnership in child protection. This research study compares two types of Child Protection Committees. Area Child Protection Committees were first established nationally in 1974 and later formulized under the first *Working Together* (DOH, 1986). They are seen as providing a joint forum for developing, monitoring and reviewing child protection policies. As was vividly illustrated by the Cleveland Enquiry, effective partnership between agencies is central to effective child protection:

> No single agency – Health, Social Services, Police or voluntary organization has the pre-eminent responsibility in the assessment of child abuse... careful consideration must be given to the detail of working arrangements between doctors, nurses, social workers, police, teachers, staff of voluntary organizations...
>
> (Butler Sloss, 1988)

The second paper by Professor Colin Pritchard, also of the University of Southampton, paints an optimistic picture on the progress made in this country in delivering child protection services. Professor Pritchard argues that the ultimate demonstration of effective partnership in child protection is the reduction in the number of children who die as a result of abuse. Between 1973-91 substantial falls were found in the infant child homicide rate in this country. He demonstrates that when these figures were compared with every developed western country, the biggest improvements were in the United Kingdom.

PARTNERSHIP: DEVELOPING JOINT AGENCY POLICIES FOR CHILD PROTECTION

Jackie Powell and Elizabeth Marks

Introduction

Whilst the Children Act 1989 has been seen by many as the most important piece of legislation relating to children this century, some commentators have been rather more critical of its ability to promote partnerships between local authorities and families. Holman (1992) suggests that the Act is fundamentally flawed in this respect and that families have only a limited involvement in decisions about their lives. One area where families might have a greater involvement is through their attendance at case conferences. Arguably, parental participation should allow parents some influence in the decision-making process. Can this be seen as evidence of partnership?

A recent study of 65 child protection conferences, undertaken in Gloucestershire (Burns, 1991), indicated that the quality of information for risk assessment had improved and that the majority of professionals and family members felt able to say that all they wanted to in the conference arena. In the context of giving firm support to the policy of parental participation, the study also suggested that greater use could be made of the Area Child Protection Committee (ACPC) in emphasising the inter-agency nature of the case conference. For example, using ACPC notepaper to invite parents to case conferences, thus indicating the inter-disciplinary nature of the meeting. The role of the ACPC in promoting inter-agency co-operation has also been highlighted in a study by Luckham and Golding (1989). They argued the need for a more active role for ACPCs in the monitoring of case conferences and in ensuring an acceptable level of parental involvement.

Area Child Protection Committees (ACPCs), first established in 1974 following the Maria Colwell Inquiry, are seen as providing a joint forum for developing, monitoring and reviewing child protection policies. However, a recent analysis of Child Abuse Inquiries (DOH, 1991: Study of Inquiry Report 1980-89) identified a number of problems related to the role of ACPCs. For example, the Cleveland Report described how, through lack of senior management agreement, the ACPC failed to provide an effective forum for the co-ordination of child protection work at street level.

Working Together (DOH, 1991: *Working Together under the Children Act 1989*), jointly prepared by the Department of Health, the Home Office, the Department of Education and Science, and the Welsh Office, made clear recommendations for a number of developments aimed at making inter-professional and inter-agency co-operation and communication more effective. The ACPC is described in some detail in Part 2 of the document and a number of recommendations regarding accountability, organization, funding, management information, and reporting systems are outlined. However, research literature on ACPCs is very limited and there is a need to know more about how these groups are formed, the nature of their membership and how they function. Drawing on a recent study of Child Protection Committees in one shire county (Powell et al., 1992), this paper describes the operation of these inter-agency arrangements and discusses them in the context of developing inter-agency practice at a policy-forming level.

The study

Working Together (DOH, 1991: Working together under the Children Act 1989) generally assumed that one ACPC would cover the area served by one local authority social services department, together with all the police or district health authorities or parts of them within that local authority's boundary. However, in the Hampshire context, in addition to the ACPC which met twice a year, there were four District Child Protection Committees (DCPCs). The latter had no formal structural links with the county-wide ACPC. In the light of the guidelines in the Department of Health's 'Working Together', two of the four DCPCs (those serving the northern and central parts of the county), adopted new structures and ways of working. This restructuring of Hampshire's child protection committees provided an opportunity to review these inter-agency arrangements during the period immediately following the adoption of what was seen as a new approach in the two newly established DCPCs.

The study, commissioned by Hampshire Social Services Department and the Social Services Inspectorate of the Department of Health, aimed at a comparison of these 'new' and 'old' approaches in different parts of the County. The overall focus of the work was on the contribution of the District CPCs to the development and management of a multi-agency child protection service. Using background documents such as policy papers and minutes, observation at meetings, and interviews with members, one 'new-style' DCPC and one 'old-style' DCPC were studied over a six-month period. Their respective roles and functions, memberships, contribution of members, and the actual working methods of the groups were compared.

Findings

The wider context of the District Child Protection Committee

All DCPC members interviewed expressed a general lack of clarity concerning the relationship between the DCPCs and the ACPC. All regarded this as an issue which needed further clarification; it was seen as having contributed to a lack of effectiveness of the DCPCs in the past. In some ways, however, the relationship between the DCPCs and the ACPC had become more problematic under the new arrangements, as the new DCPC was perceived by its members as having a more influential role than previously.

There was a shared view that the Chairs of the four DCPCs should also be members of the ACPC, and it was reported that this issue had now been taken up with the Assistant Director with County-wide special responsibility for children and families. At present, any representation from the DCPCs at the ACPC was coincidental, although all of those interviewed knew who the ACPC representative for their agency was.

There was general agreement amongst all those interviewed that the ACPC should be the overall policy making group, giving direction to and seeking information from the DCPCs. The relationship between the four DCPCs also appeared unclear to those members of the two DCPCs who were interviewed. None of our respondents were aware of any formal links between the DCPCs. Some of those who were members of more than one DCPC assumed there was contact, but could give no evidence for this view. Several members saw the need to establish more formal links between the four DCPCs, in order to look at standardizing and improving child protection practice and to avoid duplication.

The SSD's Child Protection Adviser, who was headquarters-based, attended each of the four DCPCs and the ACPC. He was identified by all DCPC members as having a crucial role in linking the four DCPCs and the ACPC. His attendance at each of these committees provided a common thread and continuity in the overall system, although there was some uncertainty about whether he provided an exclusively SSD or an inter-agency link. SSD representatives, particularly the two DCPC Chairs, saw the Adviser's role as one of providing support, advice, and information on child protection issues to the committee as a whole, but especially to the Chair of each DCPC.

Committee membership

Both committees underwent changes in SSD membership following the reorganization and decentralization of the Department. The chair of each DCPC was taken over by the Assistant Director with overall management responsibility for the relevant District, replacing the Assistant

Director with County-wide responsibility for children and families, who had previously chaired all the DCPCs. The roles and responsibilities of both the Chairs and of the SSD Area Manager representatives were similar for each DCPC under the newly devolved structure.

Differences between the two DCPCs were more evident in terms of both the level and type of representation from other agencies on these committees. The new style DCPC had higher levels of senior management representation. Only some of the individuals concerned had professional status and/or a degree of child protection expertise. The old style DCPC had higher levels of professional representation, including a multiplicity of professional groups from both the Health Authority and the Education Service.

Roles of individual members of District Child Protection Committees

The range of perceptions held by the different members of the two DCPCs studied largely reflected their different roles and their levels of input within their own organizations or agencies. Each member recognized their own contribution in one or more areas: the development of inter-agency policy and procedures, resource allocation, or child protection knowledge and expertise. Senior managers, more evident on the 'new' DCPC, generally saw themselves as making a contribution towards developing and managing inter-agency policy and procedures, although those without some relevant professional background or knowledge of child protection issues expressed some uncertainty about their being the most appropriate choice of agency representative. An emphasis on the practitioner perspective was more evident in the views expressed by members of the 'old' DCPC. This was not necessarily regarded as an alternative to the manager's perspective, but it certainly was seen as a necessary counter-balance.

Operation of District Child Protection Committees

There was general agreement that the DCPCs currently provided opportunities for the sharing of issues and concerns, and for professional networking. There was also agreement over the potential role of the DCPC in the monitoring of practice and procedures, in identifying District needs and trends, and in clarifying local issues and concerns, all of which were important in the development of child protection policy and practice. SSD representatives, in particular, saw the DCPC as providing an interface between policy and practice, through the development of links with both local inter-agency 'core groups' of professionals/front-line managers and the ACPC.

Members of the 'old' DCPC had a stronger sense of the committee as a 'talking shop', and as 'going nowhere', although there had been some change in membership with the reorganization and decentralization of the Social Services Department. Members of the new DCPC in the north of the County were generally more optimistic, although cautious, about the role of the DCPC as an active forum for the development of policy and procedures. These differences of view broadly reflected the membership of the two DCPCs, with the old style DCPC seen as primarily a senior practitioners' group and the new style DCPC as a senior managers' group. However, the potential role of the DCPC in integrating these two perspectives was also acknowledged by respondents, particularly when discussing the need for achieving greater clarity about the relationship between the DCPCs and the ACPC.

Discussion of findings

This study was set up to compare 'old' and 'new' approaches in Hampshire to the operation and role of DCPCs, and the various contributions of their members. Although a number of differences were identified, primarily in terms of membership and representation, there were striking similarities between the two DCPCs studied in respect of their relationship to other parts of the system of inter-agency arrangements for the protection of children from abuse.

Similar views on their respective individual roles were expressed by the SSD representatives on both the 'old' and 'new' DCPCs. Differences of view were more evident among members of other agencies on the DCPCs studied. As a broad generalization, the old style DCPC representatives emphasized the 'senior practitioner perspective', described as being in touch with child protection practice but carrying a District-wide overview. The membership of the committee was large, with several representatives from both Health and Education, each with somewhat different views. By comparison, the new style DCPC had a smaller membership, with only one representative from each of the two Health Authorities and Education. Although there were differences of view about who might be the most appropriate representative from Health, those attending were of senior status in their own agency. In this respect, these representatives came close to fulfilling the recommendation contained in *Working Together* that:

> Senior managers... should have sufficient authority... to speak on their agencies' behalf and to make decisions to an agreed level without referral to the appointees' agencies.
>
> (*Working Together*, DoH, 1991, p. 6)

The way that the old DCPC was perceived as a useful 'talking shop', but largely ineffectual must relate, at least in part, to its large membership and its multiplicity of intra- as well as inter-disciplinary views. Findings from this study indicate the need for agency representation and membership of the DCPCs to be stated clearly, with particular reference to delegated authority and an acknowledged inter-agency role. Nevertheless, the value of a forum for inter-agency networking at this level should not be underestimated.

However, as this study reveals, the appointment of senior officers and/or senior professionals to the DCPC was not the only issue which needed careful attention if these committees were to operate effectively. There was broad agreement across both DCPC memberships on the important role of these District Committees, and on the need for greater clarity concerning their relationships with other parts of the inter-agency child protection system. Although members of the 'new' DCPC were more optimistic about the potentially active role that this committee might play, they were, if anything, more critical than their colleagues elsewhere of the current arrangements whereby the DCPC has no formal channels of communication with the ACPC.

SSD representatives interviewed were particularly aware of the need to establish links between the DCPC and ACPC, if, as they described it, the interface between operations and strategy was to be bridged and the contribution of the DCPC in managing inter-agency policy was to be effective. For either new or old DCPCs to make any significant contribution to policy formulation, clear lines and patterns of communication are needed between the ACPC and the DCPCs.

Equally important are the links that DCPCs maintain with practice issues. The links which had been achieved through the representation of 'the core group of professionals' on Child Protection Conferences on the 'new' DCPC were seen as progress in this area. The likelihood that a similar arrangement would be introduced on the 'old' DCPC was also widely supported. In addition to representation of 'the core team', the role of the DCPC at the interface between strategy and operations could be further consolidated through the wider use of working groups, as outlined in *Working Together* (DOH, 1991).

The Chair of the Child Protection Conference, who must be a member of SSD staff, has been the representative of 'the core team' on the DCPCs. Whether it is always appropriate for the Chair of the local Conferences to be on the DCPC needs further consideration. Other members of 'the core team' may be equally well placed in making a contribution in the DCPC forum. Although the SSD is the lead agency in child protection, the possible over-representation of this one agency in inter-agency contexts needs to be constantly examined.

The Chair of the DCPC has a key role in the effective functioning of the committee. His or her ability to chair meetings, ensuring that an adequate hearing is given to all agency perspectives represented and a negotiated inter-agency view achieved, is a formidable task. *Working Together* states that:

(The Chair of the ACPC) should possess knowledge and experience of child protection work in addition to chairing skills.

(Working Together, DOH, 1991, p. 6)

In addition to these skills, it seems important that the appointment of Chairs of DCPCs should also be made on the basis of knowledge and experience of inter-agency and inter-disciplinary work. Although the SSD is the lead agency in child protection and has lead responsibility for the appointment of the Chair of the ACPC, it is important to recognize that in working together, all the agencies involved can make a significant contribution to the management of inter-agency policy, procedures and practice. The possibility of the Chairs of DCPCs being taken on a rotating basis by the core agencies involved would be one way of acknowledging this.

As a source of knowledge and experience of child protection work, the role of the SSD's County-wide Child Protection Adviser in this context appeared to be important, both specifically in relation to the Chair and generally with regard to the wider committee. However, the role and tasks of the Child Protection Adviser in relation to the ACPC and DCPCs as inter-agency committees need to be clearly stated and given adequate agency support.

In order to achieve the level of inter-agency co-operation, and in particular inter-agency management, envisaged in *Working Together* (DOH, 1991), it is necessary for each agency to take both individual and collective responsibility for establishing and maintaining the necessary inter-agency arrangements. An important part of this ongoing task is the development of a shared understanding of the importance of co-operation at all levels between the many agencies concerned with the protection of children.

Although there was some reference to the value of meeting colleagues from other agencies, little explicit comment was made concerning inter-agency working *per se*, or on the need to develop specific skills in inter-agency management. A lack of knowledge about other agencies' contributions and the specific roles of their representatives on the DCPC was noted by some committee members. An attempt to increase awareness of other agencies' perspectives and practices could provide an important first step towards the development of more effective management of a multi-agency child protection service at this level of operation.

Concluding comments

The study presented here has focused on issues concerned with promoting partnership between agencies at a policy rather than practice level, highlighting the need for inter-disciplinary and inter-agency work at several levels. Child Protection Committees have a major role in managing inter-agency arrangements and developing joint agency policies. Effective partnerships at this level can, and should provide a model of good practice for adoption at all levels of inter-agency practice. This has been clearly identified at national level.

> Co-operation at the individual case level needs to be supported by joint agency and management policies for child protection.
>
> (*Working Together*, DOH, 1991, p. 5)

In the context of this study, the DCPC plays an important part in promoting partnerships at a management and policy-forming level in order to promote and support partnerships between agencies at 'street level', and partnership developments between agencies and families.

Considerable attention has been paid to the development of inter-agency training to promote effective inter-agency practice. There is however, little acknowledgement of the need to develop skills in joint agency management, policy development, monitoring and review. As this study has shown, a considerable range of skills are required to work effectively at this level of inter-agency co-operation. There is a clear need for the development of appropriate training opportunities for members of the DCPCs, in order that they can, both individually and collectively, carry out the tasks expected of them.

A topic of much debate for participants in this study was the need for a clear policy and guidelines concerning the involvement of parents at case conferences. DCPCs, with formally established links with practice issues via representatives from 'the core team', and with clear channels of communication with the ACPC, appear ideally placed to play an important role in this area. Both the development of joint policies and the improvement of inter-agency practice should substantially influence the nature and focus of child protection work and hopefully, contribute to a more informed understanding of the complexities involved in creating partnerships in practice.

PARTNERSHIP AND CHILD PROTECTION: EVIDENCE OF EFFECTIVE CHILD PROTECTION 1973-1991 WITH SPECIAL REFERENCE TO BRITAIN AND THE USA

Colin Pritchard

Introduction

The theme of partnership in child protection is now accepted as central to any effective service (DHSS, 1986, *Working Together*). It should be remembered however, how recent is the awareness of child abuse. When

Kempe et al (1962) first used the term 'battered babies', many in Britain put it down to American hyperbole, as we felt confident that our infanticide laws, associated with puerperal psychosis, were the most positive response to this apparently rare phenomena. In 1973 the Maria Colwell tragedy shattered this professional innocence, and subsequent enquiries not only led towards a concept of partnership (Butler-Sloss, 1988), but also to question, at the heart of public concern, of how effective are our child protective services and how can this be measured?

The consequences of child abuse can range not only from the immediate distress and severe physical damage (Lynch, 1988, Calami & Franchi, 1987), but on to psycho-social problems in adulthood (Rogers et al., 1989, Pritchard et al., 1993), and further child abuse in the next generation (Oliver, 1988, Egeland, 1988, Pritchard, 1991). It is also increasingly associated with subsequent adult psychiatric disturbance (Schaffer et al., 1988; Sheldon, 1988; Van Egmond & Jonker, 1988; Rose, 1991). At the extreme, it can mean the death of the baby or infant (Kempe & Helfer, 1981; Lynch, 1988; Goetting, 1990).

A number of studies have showed that 90% plus of all baby/infant homicide are predominately, though not all, the result of parental or intra-familial violence (Scott, 1973; D'Orban, 1979; Resnick, 1980; Bourget & Bradford, 1990; Somander & Rammer, 1991), and are often linked to family patterns found to be associated with child abuse (Herrenkohl & Herrenkohl, 1983; Oates, 1984; Egeland et al., 1987). However, older child homicide, 5-14 years, increasingly involves non-family assailants and this is one reason for focusing upon baby and infant deaths. The other is the startling fact that unlike most forms of violent death, where the highest proportional rate is found amongst young men 18-24, *babies* are, per population, the most frequent victims of murder. Thus homicide rates can be seen as the extreme end of the continuum of child maltreatment.

How therefore, in our partnerships, can we demonstrate successful prevention? By reversing the question and measuring failure, i.e. the extreme consequence, in the children's homicide rates, as a paradoxical indicator of effective protection. This does not mean we ignore all non-fatal abuse or neglect, but the national homicide rate shows whether or not we influence the extreme outcomes.

This reflects the epidemiological tradition of Durkheim (1952), that significant variations in mortality rates may reflect change in social cohesion, a concept which has won broad acceptance (Berrios & Mohanna, 1990). The likely major environmental change which might be reflected in baby/infant homicide, would be poverty, as increases in levels of child abuse have been associated with worsening poor economic circumstances (Steinberg et al., 1981; Madge, 1983; Krugman et al., 1986; McLoyd, 1990). Nevertheless, substantial changes in baby/infant murder are one indicator of improvement or deterioration in a society's ability to protect its children.

The use of the baby/infant homicide rate as a comparative baseline is a rigorous criteria, but mortality rates have been validated as a method to gauge societal changes in a range of pathologies (e.g. Platt, 1984; Bodmer, 1988; Fitzpatrick, 1989; W.H.O., 1990). Also the use of mortality statistics resolves some of the often sterile debate about defining child abuse, as it is the outermost end of the continuum, and is at the heart of the long-standing concern about how effective is our child protection service (Parker et al., 1991).

The weakness in any epidemiological approach however, are the questions which can not be answered. For example, little can be revealed about individuals, or the form which the child protection may have taken, or to what extent improvements in medical technology influenced subsequent death rates over time. Notwithstanding, the strategy permits both national and inter-national macro comparisons to be made, providing data to facilitate the exploration of policy and practice.

In the final analysis, the degree to which the general public and politicians can have confidence in our ability to protect the most vulnerable is how the disciplines will be judged, and despite the crude political scapegoating that we have come to expect (Franklin & Parton, 1991), it is perhaps the judgement we would wish to accept.

Explanation of source of data and analysis

A brief outline of the source of the data is necessary, because of the undoubted difficulties, and even controversy, which surrounds research in this field (Parker et al., 1991; Ward & Jackson, 1991; Creighton, 1993), and to provide the reader with information to judge whether the case has been made. All data is taken from the World Health Organization 'Annual Statistics' (1973-1993). The age bands examined are 'babies' i.e. under 1 year old; 'infants' 1-4 years, and 'child' deaths, 5-14 years. Apart from exploring the actual number of UK homicides for each age band, we use death rates per million population, not absolute numbers for the intra and inter-national comparisons. This allows us to compare a nation's rate over time, and to compare countries of different populations. Also there is little point in making a direct comparison between national rates because they may be influenced by varied recording systems, so a country is first compared against itself, and any changes over time are noted.

Despite the massive media concern, baby and infant murders, compared say with their deaths on the road, are relatively small. This means however, that slight changes in a year may disproportionately effect the rates, so to reduce the influence of one year, the total for *two* baseline years, 1973 and 1974, are used to compare the index years of 1990 and 1991. From this we calculate an index of change. If there was no variation between the years the index would be 100, whilst a decline of 10%

would be 090, but a rise of 10% would make the index 110. The *index of change* between countries are then compared, which resolves the problem of differences in a country's recording system, as a country is compared against itself before making an international comparison. This method has been successfully applied across a number of different fields (Pritchard, 1992a,b,c, 1993a) and largely resolves the problems inherent in international comparisons (Gelles & Edfeldt, 1986).

The baseline year of comparison was the year of the oil-crisis in 1973, since which time unemployment has been endemic, and there is evidence of an association with child abuse and negative socio-economic circumstance (e.g Steinberg et al., 1981; Krugman et al., 1986; McLoyd, 1990). Perhaps more important, in view of the theme of partnership, it was the year of the Maria Colwell inquiry.

It is however, acknowledged that this is not a perfect method and that cross national comparisons, in particular, are fraught with methodological issues (Gelles & Edfeldt, 1986), not least those problems surrounding the *definition* of child abuse. For us, however, a dead child is an unequivocal measure, though it is possible that there might be an under-reporting because of parental covert action, or reluctance on the part of professionals to make such judgements.

Finally, it must be repeated that this epidemiological approach which uses homicide as a paradoxical indicator of successful child protection, can say little about the 'content' or 'process' of the services. Hopefully what it can do is provide a measure which, as will be seen, gives grounds for encouragement, and which should place the media hyped failures into better perspective.

In respect to gender and homicide in the developed world, male adult murders are at about twice the rate for that of women (WHO, 1993). However, in regard to baby deaths, females scored higher in England and Wales on eight occasions and ten in Scotland over the period. Internationally, out of a possible 108 combinations by country, gender and age groups, males had a higher score than females a third of the time, females a third, and the remainder were tied. Hence the rationale for not separating out gender in the analysis, especially bearing in mind the small numbers involved.

The findings

To give an indication of the general level of homicide rate in the Anglo-Welsh population, Table 6.1 overleaf gives the actual homicide deaths, in each age band, and calculates an index of change between 1973/74 and 1990/91.

Despite the media image of an increasingly violent society, murder has fallen, in every age band, except the 45-54 group. As this later rose

Table 6.1
England & Wales
Homicide by age bands – ratio of change 1973/74 – 1990/91

Year	All	<1	1-4	5-14	15-24	25-34	35-44	45-54	55-64	65-74	75+
1973	448	40	34	28	88	81	49	40	36	32	20
1974	318	35	40	31	74	48	56	26	24	25	20
73/74	766	75	74	59	162	129	105	66	60	57	40
1990	257	8	17	11	40	55	36	35	26	16	13
1991	273	11	16	14	38	50	47	33	23	25	16
90/91	530	19	33	25	78	50	83	68	49	41	29
Change											
Ratio	069	025	045	042	048	081	079	103	082	072	073

Table 6.2
Annual baby, infant & child homicides United Kingdom
(actual deaths)

Year	Baby <1	Infant 1-4	Child 5-14	Total 0-14 yrs
1973	46	39	32	117
1974	37	41	34	112
1975	39	34	39	112
1976	42	28	35	105
1977	25	34	35	94
1978	31	42	31	104
1979	40	33	35	108
1980	18	18	20	56
1981*	14	8	15	37
1982*	14	22	22	58
1983	18	28	13	59
1984	11	28	22	61
1985	14	28	20	62
1986	18	10	21	49
1987	11	21	14	46
1988	23	15	18	56
1989	23	14	18	55
1990	8	19	14	41
1991	15	21	15	51
Combined 1973/74	83	80	66	229
Combined 1990/91	23	40	29	92
Index of Change	028	050	044	040

[* Northern Ireland's rates were not available]

by only an equivalent of 3% it would not be considered substantial, especially bearing in mind the relatively small numbers. For interest, the changes in the annual homicides of the United Kingdom 1973-1991 are illustrated in Table 6.2

However, it is noteworthy that the biggest reductions were for the baby and infant age bands. Actual deaths do not of course, take into account population variations, hence the rationale of using rates per million.

It can be seen that over the period there has been a marked fall in children's homicide, equivalent to a 72% fall in baby murders in the United Kingdom between 1973 and 1991.

However, and this must be stressed, in terms of *proportion* of deaths per population, except for Northern Ireland, more babies are murdered than any other age band in the rest of the U.K.

A Western world comparison

To determine how relevant these improvements are, an international comparison is offered and Table 6.3 provides data on the other Western countries with which to compare the British results. The calculations are presented in a 'league table', showing the rank order of improvements in the index of overall baby to child deaths (0-14 years), from 1973/74 to the latest year figures available, 1990/91s.

Two general points should be noted; first there is a wide range of baby and total death rates between countries, many of which have changed substantially over the past decade or so; second, in almost all countries, the homicide rate is higher amongst babies than any other age band. It is approximately three or four times the infant level, which in turn, is about twice the rate of child (5-14) deaths (W.H.O., 1973-1993). This dramatically highlights the vulnerability of babies.

In 1973-1974, before child abuse was widely recognized, nine countries had a total mortality rate of 100+ child homicide per million. These were; Japan (230), Austria (188), USA (187), West Germany (158), England and Wales (147), Scotland (136), New Zealand (118), Finland and Switzerland (114) each. Conversely, seven countries had total rates of less than 30 per million; Spain (10), Ireland (18), Portugal (22), Italy (26), Greece (28), and Sweden (29). Thus it might be said that the 'child killers' were predominately the English and German speaking countries, and the Anglo-Welsh were the fourth worst in the western world. Not an enviable position to hold.

By 1990/91 there were interesting changes, Japan at 96 no longer had the highest total rate, but surprisingly this dubious distinction went to the United States at 244! The high for New Zealand, at 200 per million, might be partly explained by the impact that small changes have upon countries with small populations, but the USA figures, whilst following

Table 6.3
Annual average murder and age bands 1973/74 and 1990/91
(rates per million)

	Years	Babies	Infants	5-14	0-14	Index of Change
Greece	73/74	22	2	4	28	
	89/90	0	0	1	1	004
England/Wales	73/74	114	25	8	147	
	90/91	27	13	4	39	027
Japan	73/74	166	48.	16	230	
	90/91	73	15	8	96	042
Switzerland	73/74	96	9	9	114	
	90/91	24	23	7	54	047
W Germany	73/74	125	23	10	158	
	89/90	68	12	6	86	054
Italy	73/74	17	4	5	26	
	88/90	6	5	5	16	062
Scotland	73/74	110	18	8	136	
	90/91	58	27	6	91	067
Finland	73/74	86	20	8	114	
	90/91	60	8	8	76	067
Denmark	73/74	57	18	13	88	
	90/91	46	13	6	65	074
Norway	73/74	32	0	3	35	
	90/91	17	9	2	28	080
Austria	73/74	166	14	8	188	
	90/91	118	23	17	158	084
Netherlands	73/74	31	4	4	39	
	89/90	20	12	3	35	090
Spain	73/74	8	1	1	10	
	88/89	3	3	3	9	090
Ireland	73/74	15	0	3	18	
	89/90	18	0	0	18	100
Australia	73/74	49	24	13	86	
	87/88	74	18	11	103	120
France	73/74	34	11	4	49	
	89/90	39	14	7	60	122
U.S.A.	73/74	129	47	11	187	
	88/89	163	53	28	244	130
Sweden	73/74	0	21	8	29	
	88/89	27	10	5	42	145
N.Zealand	73/74	84		29	5	118
	88/89	173	15	12	200	169
Belgium	73/74	32	9	6	47	
	86/87	86	26	14	126	268
Portugal	73/74	18		0	4	22
	90/91	103	8	4	115	523

a recent noted trend (Pritchard, 1993b), were frankly startling and merit later discussion.

The other countries which exceeded composite 100+ rates included; Austria (158), Belgium (126), Portugal (115) and Australia (103). The bottom seven were Greece, of course, with only 1 – more of that result in a moment – Spain (9), Italy (16), Ireland (18), Norway (28), Netherlands (35) and England and Wales at 39. Thus England and Wales, from being fourth highest, fell to seventh lowest.

It must be stressed however, that what is crucial in international comparisons is not the differential rates of countries, but rather how a country changes over time when measured against itself, and how this figure varies between the nations. Greece's coming top follows a marked trend over the past five years, though it must be remembered that they, and Portugal, have undergone major post-revolutionary changes which may have accounted for marked variations in their statistics over the period (WHO, 1973-1991). What is clear, with both countries, is that they have had the largest actual and proportional reduction in infant mortality overall, although they had the highest rate pre-membership of the European Community.

Nonetheless, on both the actual and proportional calculations, England and Wales showed remarkable improvement, with Scotland being equal seventh best in the twenty-two western developed nations.

Generally however, it is good to record that thirteen western countries had reduced their over-all deaths by at least an equivalent of 10%+, with England and Wales leading the improvements in countries with large populations. In times when the public service is taught to look at industry as a model for its activities, it is pleasing to see Japan and West Germany behind Britain, which even if we had included the UK figures, would still have been the case.

Discussion

It is acknowledged that a study based upon aggregated data has a number of limitations. For example, nothing can be said about either individuals or what, if any, was the nature of the type of intervention which may have influenced the differential outcomes within and between countries. The issue of 'reporting' can not be completely resolved, for whilst there is no firm indication from the W.H.O sources that reporting methods/systems have been altered, there is no way we can prove or disprove this 'negative'. All that can be addressed is the direction of change within and between national mortalities.

The analysis rests upon the assumption that children's homicide is the extreme consequence of abuse associated with intra-family violence (Bourget & Bradford, 1990, Somander & Rammer, 1991). There is support for this proposition inherent in the national studies which link death-to-cases of abuse ratios (USDHHS, 1981, ACCP, 1986), yet even if this assumption was not accepted, the substantial changes in British baby homicide still require some explanation.

There were two major, perhaps surprising, findings in this analysis. First, apart from Greece, England & Wales at 027, the United Kingdom has a whole, at 040, had the largest reduction of children's homicides in the Western world. Second, the children's murder rate increased by 34% in America, and only four other countries had greater proportional increases in baby deaths, though had all started from a much lower base-rate. In terms of the archetypal child abuse death, that of babies, the actual number almost doubled, rising from 327 to 650, an increase of 99%!

Whilst bearing in mind the limits of aggregated data, what may account for the improvements in the British situation and the deterioration in America?

Firstly, that the improvements in the British situation were due to a recording artifact, and that there has been little real change, was an argument put by Creighton (1993). She pointed out that there had been an alteration of the recording in 1978, when the use of the 'undetermined death' category was extended in Britain. She argued that this would obliterate the improvements, because courts would be more likely to use the more equivocal 'decision' about death, rather than having to prove homicide. This may be so. However, it assumes that the majority of 'undetermined deaths' were the result of abuse – a highly questionable position, for whilst there may have been a element of this in the earlier years, it is suggested that ALL involved with children more recently have never been more aware of the ramifications of child abuse, and therefore there would be a far greater recognition of the possibility of any deaths being deliberate. It would also mean that assailants were, in face of increased vigilance, more able to hide from alerted professionals. Whilst Creighton is right to be concerned that 'false' figures may lure us to be complacent, she appears to ignore evidence of the positive affect of the child protection services, seen in her and the NSPCC's worry about an apparent fall in the number of 'Child Protection Register' cases. But Little & Gibbons (1992) in an ingenious analysis of all local authorities, show that there is a degree of consistency in the final figures, which strongly points towards intervention heading-off the need for registration.

The Creighton argument is important, but is answered more fully elsewhere (Pritchard, 1993c). Sufficient to say that if we did calculate as Creighton advised, ignoring the Greek result, then sadly Britain would no longer head 'the league' of reduction of children homicide. We would be second to Japan, and the rate of improvement would only exceed 50%! If cancer deaths were reduced by such a level, the media bells would be almost deafening.

However, let us be cautious, another factor may be that child abuse deaths are being hid in accidents. Again this is unlikely, not only because of alerted professionals, but more importantly, through the evidence that accident deaths have halved throughout most of the western world (WHO, 1973-1993), Pritchard, 1992b).

One other factor comes to mind, that of 'cot deaths', or Sudden Infant Death Syndrome (SIDS). Newlands & Emery (1991) noted a higher incidence of SIDS amongst families known to a Social Service Department. However (and this demands a study on its own), this is a very dangerous assumption because some of the socio-economic and embryological factors associated with SIDS are linked to poverty, which crosses over into the SSD caseload. It may well be the case that some S.I.D.S. are associated with neglect, but frankly the case is not proven, and certainly not to the extent of the changes in SIDS, both in Britain and the western world (Pritchard & Hayes, 1993). For example, in a British study under preparation within a falling infant mortality rate, 26,000 babies died in 1970 and 1971, but less than 11,000 by 1990/91. In 1970/71, 3% of the deaths were classified as unknown i.e. 'ill-defined death', yet by the later period they had risen to 20%, i.e. 2,210 (Pritchard, 1993d), a rise that has followed major strides in medical diagnostics. Such increases clearly lie outside the 'neglect' field, and point towards wider environmental factors such as ' Inter-Uterine Growth Retardation' (Hinchcliff et al., 1993), and *probably* some multi-variate environmental factor (Pritchard & Hayes, 1993).

On balance therefore it is claimed that the most probable reason for the improvement in British children's homicide rates is due to improved child protection.

However, before we congratulate ourselves there are reasons for caution, especially when budgets allocated to the disciplines of the protective services are at possible risk. It is for this reason we spend a little time considering the surprising, indeed alarming results from the USA. It had been *expected* that there would have been reductions in American children's mortality because of the growing evidence of improving child protection (e.g. Burch & Mohr, 1980; Zimrin, 1984; Rowe, 1985; Pritchard, 1991), and because the USA had led to world in identifying and understanding child abuse (e.g. Kempe et al., 1962; Finkel, 1987; Egeland et al., 1987).

We have reviewed the possible methodological factors which might explain these USA findings elsewhere (Pritchard, 1993a), and they appear valid. The question is therefore, why should the richest and most professionally advanced country in the world fall behind in a service in which they led everyone else?

It seems unlikely that was because of a reduced competence of the USA child protective services, as America has seminal international figures who alerted and taught the rest of us about child abuse (e.g.

Garabino, 1986; Egeland et al., 1987; Baird et al., 1988). It is suggested therefore, that the current American children's services were overwhelmed for some reason.

It is known that child abuse is associated with negative socio-economic circumstances, (Steinberg et al., 1981; Madge, 1983; Krugman et al., 1986; Gelles, 1989; McLloyd, 1990), and here may lie the clue . Though a socio-economic explanation of the American results must remain conjectural, in the recession of the 1980s which effected almost every developed nation, the only country to de facto to reduce their *poverty compensatory* welfare services was the U.S.A, despite the fact there was a measured increase in relative poverty (MacFate et al., 1991). It *may* be therefore, that the 'poverty dimension', associated with unemployment, *might* have been a contributory factor in the worsening situation of American child homicides, in effect, over-loading a service who could not respond to the extra burden?

Obviously, whilst the vast majority of poor people do not neglect or damage their children, the link between economic deprivation and child abuse can not be gainsaid. And, perhaps more telling, this socio-economic emphasis is consistent with other American negative social indices, reflected in deteriorating mortality statistics. For example, compared to most western countries, American youth suicide has, like the British, Canadian and Australasian, worsened considerably (Rotherum-Borus, 1989; Pritchard, 1992c, 1992d). In addition there has been significant rises in suicide amongst elderly Americans, which, proportionately, was the worst in the developed world. The American situation is analyzed in greater detail elsewhere (Pritchard, 1993a, d) but it is the lesson for Britain which is important.

Whilst not ignoring the multiplicity of other possible etiological contributory elements, for example drug and alcohol abuse (Roberts, 1988; Pritchard et al., 1990, 1993), or the special psychiatric factors associated with children's homicide (Scott, 1973; D'Orban, 1979; Resnick, 1980; Prins, 1986,1988), the dismemberment and reduction of a range of welfare services in North America throughout the 1980s, may well be a key reason for their surprising deterioration.

Consequently, it is feared that the major improvement of British child protection may be in jeopardy from possible reductions of welfare services, reductions which fail to measure the accumulative outcome of failure to reach and sustain vulnerable people. Sadly, there is no doubt that since 1987, there have been proportional planned reductions in British welfare services, relative to the level of G.D.P. devoted to the social budgets (McFate et al., 1991; Pritchard, 1992e). Politicians may relate grandiose numbers, but without proper baselines with which to compare the apparent increases, it is so much party political hyperbole. It is feared that these improvement s might be at risk from the planned reduction of GDP devoted to the NHS and Community Care services.

78

But let us end positively. There is evidence from many areas of practice, that social work does positively influence the lives of many of our most disadvantaged and disturbed citizens. That we can compensate and ameliorate some of the worst impacts of psycho-social deprivation. Not enough perhaps, certainly in the areas of the socio-economic, but sufficient to reach people who feel despairing and excluded. Providing we maximize ALL our professional expertise in the constant pursuit of excellence, than we can begin to explain, prevent and reverse the ultimate abuse of children.

Summary

Partnership is crucial to effective work, but how can we demonstrate successful prevention when the extremes of child abuse can end with a dead child? This chapter offers an epidemiological solution to the question of evaluation. The vast majority of baby/infant homicide are known to be intra-familial, any substantial variation therefore points to changes in levels of child abuse. Consequently, children's homicide can be a paradoxical indicator of the effectiveness of a country's child protection. This is shown in an analysis of baby/infant murder between 1973-91. Whilst all western world countries are analysed, we take a special look at the UK, which had one of the biggest reductions, and the USA, whose position worsened considerably.

It is argued that the social work and other child protection services have little to fear from evaluation, provided that high professional standards and commitment are maintained in the collaborative service of children and their families.

Acknowledgements

I am indebted to Professor D Holt, Department of Social Statistics, for his invaluable statistical advice, and to Ann Buchanan, Department of Social Work Studies, University of Southampton, for patient editorial guidance. Finally, to Claire Elizabeth Pritchard, Thames Valley University, my thanks for her conscientious archival assistance.

7 Specialist practice

This chapter looks at the work of four different specialists and highlights how working in partnership under the Children Act has come to be interpreted in each area. In the first two papers, there is a common theme of working in partnership with multi-agencies and multi-disciplines, as well as in partnership with families. In meeting child health needs, Dr Christine Smalley, consultant paediatrician in Community Child Health, outlines her service for children who are in 'need' and/or disabled. In the second section Adrian Faupel, senior educational psychologist for Hampshire, discusses his interpretation of 'partnership' when working with children and the families of children with specific educational needs, in particular emotional and behavioural difficulties. In both of these papers there is also the common theme that the parents are the experts and the most effective way of meeting the health and/or educational needs of their children is by acknowledging and working with the expertise of the parents. The third section describes the work of Scope. Scope is effectively a club for parents who have children under five who are in need. It is run by the members, who are parents, for the members. Here too is the recognition that the real experts on meeting needs are parents themselves, especially parents who may have been through many of the same hoops. The final paper looks at the representations procedure, or as it is commonly called 'the complaints procedure'. This procedure is the lynch pin to the Children Act. This paper, which is based on the workshop led by Gwen James of Voice for the Child in Care at the conference in 1992, advocates a positive view of complaints both as a way of making partnerships more equal and as a way of monitoring the services provided under the Act.

PARTNERSHIP AND CHILD HEALTH

Dr Christine Smalley

An introductory guide for the National Health Service (DOH, 1991:NHS) states eight main principles of the Act. A central principle is that parents with children in need should be helped to bring up their children themselves and this help should be provided as a service to the child and family. The principles also state that this help should be provided in partnership with parents. In giving a service, the guide says that this service should meet each child's identified needs and that it should be appropriate to the child's race, culture, religion and linguistic background. This service should also be open to an effective, independent, representations and complaints procedures and finally should draw upon effective partnership between the local authority and other agencies.

The task for Community Child Health is how to put these principles into practice.

Under the Children Act the definition for a child in need is:

(a) he is unlikely to achieve or maintain , or have the opportunity of achieving or maintaining, a reasonable standard of health or development without the provision for him of services by a local authority or,

b) his health or development is likely to be significantly impaired, or further impaired, without the provision for him of such services; or

c) he is disabled

(Children Act section 17.10)

The Community Child Health team has a role in four tasks. The first task is to *identify* children who are in need as defined above; the second major task is to *assess* these children and their individual needs, and the third task is to *provide* for these needs; the final task is to *plan* strategies for all children in need.

In undertaking these tasks, the Community Child Health team will be working in *partnership together with parents* who may be in contact with a number of agencies, and the team will be working in *partnership agency to agency*.

The following diagram highlights the many different partnership relationships that may be required to work with children in need and their families:

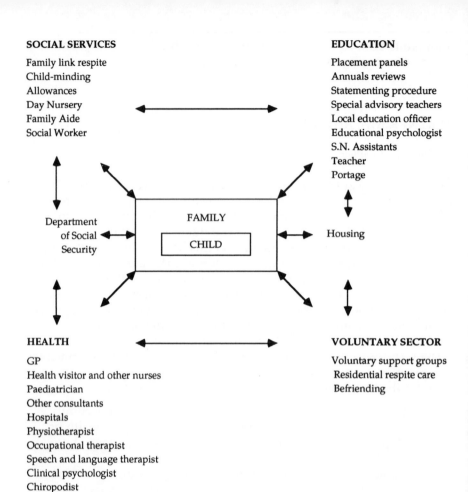

SOCIAL SERVICES

Family link respite
Child-minding
Allowances
Day Nursery
Family Aide
Social Worker

EDUCATION

Placement panels
Annuals reviews
Statementing procedure
Special advisory teachers
Local education officer
Educational psychologist
S.N. Assistants
Teacher
Portage

Department
of Social
Security

FAMILY

CHILD

Housing

HEALTH

GP
Health visitor and other nurses
Paediatrician
Other consultants
Hospitals
Physiotherapist
Occupational therapist
Speech and language therapist
Clinical psychologist
Chiropodist
Orthoptist
Seating clinic
Child guidance

VOLUNTARY SECTOR

Voluntary support groups
Residential respite care
Befriending

Figure 7.1 Partnership and child health

To begin to consider the concept of 'partnership' a definition of the word is required. In the Concise Oxford Dictionary (1975) partnership is defined as: 'the state of being a partner'. More helpfully a 'partner' is described as:

a sharer, or a person associated with others in business of which he shares risks and profits, or a wife or husband, or a companion in dance or game , or an associate with another.

All give a different perspective of a close, shared relationship, which we need to strive for constantly in our practice. Some models of practice which demonstrate working in partnership are given below.

Identification of children in need

In *Health for All Children* (Hall, 1991), Hall outlines the important role parents have in detecting the health needs of children. Parents are the experts on their child, but in order to interpret the signs and symptoms that they see daily, and to recognize those that are important, parents need information. In Southampton this is done by giving all parents the responsibility of keeping their child's health record from birth. This record also includes general information about child health. The parents are therefore the first line in the identification of children who may have special needs.

In many situations this practice is continued should the child need specialist investigation and assessment. Copies of reports are often given to parents, (e.g. at Wordsworth House, Child Development Centre, Southampton). Although initially this practice raised anxieties amongst the professionals concerned, it is now working well. The more complicated the child's health problems, the greater the benefit of parent-held information. Whenever parents hold records they have the responsibility for taking them from agency to agency, so that at each appointment there is no problem with delayed communications or missing information.

Another avenue for a identifying child in need is through the Registers held by Health, Education and Social Services. At present in Southampton these are not linked registers, but information is passed between agencies and registers with parental permission. Discussions are taking place to consider joint registers.

Further children are identified through the Homelessness Project, in particular the work at St Dismas Centre. In Southampton, large numbers of children are living in bed and breakfast accommodation. The Homelessness Project has demonstrated the value of health visitors linking with housing departments both in identifying children who have health and other needs, and in meeting these needs.

Finally, another example of working in partnership with the voluntary sector to identify children in need is via the PATCH Project (Play And Topics Concerning Health). This project targets needy communities, bringing in a 'playbus' for the children, where open parent-led discussions on child health topics can be facilitated with a health visitor.

Assessment

The Child Development Centre at Wordsworth House, with its multi-disciplinary team, is there to assess the needs of children who have or may have some disability. Parents are totally involved in the assessment process, from being present at all attendances, to full participation in the discussions and in receiving copies of reports. New ways are always being developed to cement this working partnership.

In the field of Child Protection, the community child health service have recently appointed a new senior nurse in Child Protection and a nurse trainer in Child Protection. Also a newly appointed consultant community Paediatrician has taken a lead role as senior designated doctor. These appointments should facilitate better working relationship to protect children as envisaged in *Working Together* (DOH, 1991: WT).

Assessment of the health needs of children accommodated by the Local Authority will be enhanced by the appointment of a medical advisor with specific responsibilities for these children. Such a post is high priority for development by the Community Child Health Service, and will complement the existing medical advisor role for children who are to be adopted.

Provision

An important provision for children with disabilities is the Opportunity Playgroup. These are led by parents, for parents and children, and are supported by Health, Education and Social Services. The health input is from medical officers, health visitors, physiotherapists, speech therapists and for one group, clinical psychology.

Wordsworth House, the Child Development Centre, provides ongoing support and therapy as well as assessment, for children with disability and their families. Again, joint providers are Education, Health and Social Services. Wordsworth House links widely with outside services and with parent support groups.

For children with disability who require respite care, a respite care resource panel co-ordinates entry to these services. Parents are invited to panel meetings to discuss respite requirements with representatives from the voluntary sector, health and social services. Respite facilities available are a mixture of residential and home-based provisions.

A new partnership being developed for children with severe learning difficulties or autism is the community-based team. From January 1993 two teams (one based in the City and the other in the New Forest) will be developed. Members of each core team will be a specialist nurse, a clinical psychologist and a social worker, supported by doctors, teachers and respite care providers, to give support to families of those children in need.

Planning

Future needs are co-ordinated through the Children's Joint Planning Group which includes representatives from health, education, social services and the voluntary organizations. This group is supported by 'standing' locality subgroups.

There are at present two specialist subgroups with parental representation. The first of these focuses on children with severe learning difficulties and the second on joint assessment. In the past there have also been specialist subgroups for children with chronic health needs, and children experiencing emotional and behavioural difficulties.

With the many changes in the pipeline, and the increasing demands on our services, partnership with parents, children and other agencies is going to be central to the way in which services are provided in child health in the future.

PARTNERSHIP AND CHILDREN WITH SPECIAL NEEDS IN EDUCATION

Adrian Faupel
Original recording by Sylvia Sleeman

Introduction

The welfare of children is central to the concerns of the three agencies; Health, Social Services and Education, but to achieve this core aim for each agency individually requires that they recognize that they have mutual and overlapping concerns. Poor health, for example, can undermine a child's ability to learn, and the child's physical and social environment has been shown to have strong associations with health. Given the fact that ALL children, with a minute fraction being educated at home, attend school, the relationship between Education and Health and Social Services is particularly important. At the preventative level, schools have a unique role to play in the physical and mental health of the nation and it is a very narrow, and in my view, false view of education, which sees it as being concerned solely with academic learning. Schools do, and should, play a vital part in the emotional and social development of children and young people. The quality of the peer relationships among young children is, for example, now seen as being very important, not only in significantly contributing to their emotional adjustment in childhood itself, but more importantly perhaps to their ability to form satisfactory and fulfilling relationships as adults (Parker & Asher, 1987).

There are a number of important areas where the relationship between the Children Act and educational provision is extremely close – pre-school provision, child abuse procedures, children with disabilities, and issues of attendance and truancy. This paper will examine only the

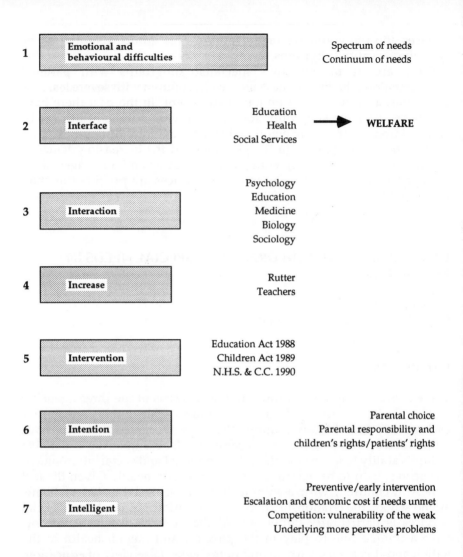

1	Emotional and behavioural difficulties	Spectrum of needs Continuum of needs
2	Interface	Education Health → WELFARE Social Services
3	Interaction	Psychology Education Medicine Biology Sociology
4	Increase	Rutter Teachers
5	Intervention	Education Act 1988 Children Act 1989 N.H.S. & C.C. 1990
6	Intention	Parental choice Parental responsibility and children's rights/patients' rights
7	Intelligent	Preventive/early intervention Escalation and economic cost if needs unmet Competition: vulnerability of the weak Underlying more pervasive problems

Figure 7.2 Partnership and children with needs in education

interface between the Children Act and the area of special educational needs stemming from emotional and behavioural difficulties (EBD). The figure above illustrates some of the issues:

Interface

Children are not made up of HEALTH, SOCIAL AND EDUCATIONAL 'components'; such divisions are solely for our bureaucratic convenience. The welfare of the child can only be achieved by maintaining a totally holistic view and all the various agencies constantly need to subordinate partial and compartmentalized perspectives to the needs of the whole child. Services have to mesh with each other, and we have indicated above how one aspect of the child's welfare and development is incomprehensible without acknowledging the interaction and interplay of many others.

Interaction

The ecological model of behaviour indicates that a child's behaviour can only be understood as being the result of the child's complex interactions with family, school and neighbourhood. Any useful understanding of such behaviour requires a thorough and detailed analysis of a whole host of factors. A number of disciplines have valid contributions to make to such an understanding – psychology, education, sociology, biology, medicine, police and the justice systems to name but the most important. We go up a blind alley if we are tempted to view the explanation of difficult behaviours as located within the child. Understanding leads to doing – and to meet these children's diverse needs requires partnership between all the diverse agencies, and not least partnership with the parents (and the child). That is by no means easy to achieve, and sadly may be becoming more difficult in present circumstances.

Increase

Some of these present circumstances seem to be responsible for increasing the amount and severity of emotional and behavioural difficulties. It is notoriously difficult to collect hard empirical data to show this is happening. The evidence there is (Rutter, 1992), and particularly the anecdotal evidence from teachers and from rates of referral etc., indicate that there has been an increase in both the numbers of children presenting with EBD and an increase in its severity. 'Partnership' with all the parties outlined above is going to become increasing important in the face of such trends.

Intervention

Society's response to the presence of EBD has been encapsulated in three important pieces of legislation; the Education Act 1988; the Children Act 1989 and the National Health and Community Care Act. All three have important consequences for children and young people experiencing emotional and behavioural difficulties. The intentions, (some might say the rhetoric), of the three Acts are clearly to be welcomed – those of the Education Act were to ensure that parents should have more choice and detailed information about the education of their children, and to enhance the quality of the education being delivered by all schools. The National Health and Community Care Act was designed to ensure that people with needs should have better service and a greater choice. The Children Act set out to ensure greater parental responsibility, to protect children from significant harm, and to ensure that the welfare of the child was paramount. However, the first two Acts are qualitatively different from the Children Act – both of them saw improvement of standards as being achieved by the use of 'market forces' and competition. In education, for example, the choice of parents will be determined by performance of schools competing with each other in the 'market place'. Unfortunately, some children are not very 'marketable', and none more so than those with emotional and behavioural difficulties. The recently documented rapid rise in exclusions from schools is a direct result of such policies and probably has nothing to do with an increase of bad behaviour within schools.

Intention

It appears increasingly the case that the declared intentions of these two Acts, and particularly of the mechanism chosen to realise these intentions, are actually at variance with the rights and 'good' of the child as embodied in the Children Act. Increasing potential choice in the Education Act 1988, whilst commendable in itself, has very serious effects on the rights and welfare of some children. Parental choice is based upon narrow and crudely defined criteria of successful schools' such as exam results and attendance rates, and the publication of 'league tables'. Difficult pupils become unwanted pupils because of their effect upon the school's position in the league table. Patient's rights in the Health Service are also based upon the right to choose, but market forces may themselves limit what there is to choose from.

The application of a market place philosophy to education is often inappropriate. The weak and the vulnerable, that is those with the greatest needs, are even further marginalized. The needs of 'minorities' become engulfed by the more powerful majority. Where does that leave partnership?

Intelligent ways forward

Preventative approaches and early intervention are seen by the professions involved as being crucial responses to special needs. But these are 'long term' benefits, difficult to 'demonstrate' and thus always coming very low on the political agenda.

The mainstream education system is currently becoming even less responsive to the needs of children with emotional and behavioural difficulties. When schools are under pressure, they tend to become less flexible, and there is in addition a potential conflict between the needs of a particular child and the way the demands of the National Curriculum are perceived. A child who has been abused may need to spend time in a social service setting, perhaps even on a daily basis. Not all schools can handle this: it is their 'system' which becomes paramount, rather than the needs of children.

Not all is gloom and doom, however. Education is indeed undergoing tremendous change. With schools having even more control over their own budgets, theoretically they can be even more flexible and creative, and indeed locally this is seen to be happening. Local partnership arrangements to meet particular needs are being developed and in one area of Hampshire, for example, a jointly managed education/social service facility 'sharing' resources under a jointly funded project leader is being piloted.

Parent power may be the mechanism which alone can force agencies with vested interests to work together. Resources will need to be increasingly pooled. So most important, perhaps is the empowering of parents, particularly those with children with emotional and behavioural difficulties, to use the already existing complaint procedures. These undoubtedly need further strengthening. However, the most important way forward to meeting the needs of all children, and especially those with EBD, is the genuine spirit of partnership between Health, Education and Social Services, which sees children as whole children and not made up of 'separable' parts.

PARENTS IN PARTNERSHIP

Geoff Poulton

Amongst the many child care specialists in our welfare society it is possible to forget the specialist skills of parents who practice child care twenty four hours a day, seven day a week, often with no time off for holidays. The growth of nine-to-five child care expertise has to some degree, eroded the confidence and devalued the expertise of parents who in the past supported each other through the day to day traumas of child rearing. In recent years, however, conscious efforts have been made to restore these supportive networks. One of the oldest of these schemes is SCOPE.

SCOPE is an independent organization which offers support for families with children under the age of five years. It is organized in Units of five or six neighbourhood groups. Each Unit has a paid co-ordinator whose work includes visiting families who have been recommended to them by health, education, social services and voluntary agencies. The families are invited to join one of the neighbourhood groups which meet on a weekly basis at places within walking distance of their homes.

In addition to the weekly group meetings, contact between families continues in their homes. SCOPE also runs a residential Family House in Southampton for members who are in need of a short break during particularly stressful times in their lives.

SCOPE has now completed seventeen years of work with families containing children under five. During this time, many hundreds of families in Hampshire have been involved in our activities as members, while the membership is continually changing. We see this as a mark of success. The aims have remained constant:

- to provide friendship and support for parents
- to build up the confidence of parents
- to gain more knowledge about the health and well-being of children and adults
- to enable parents and children to meet others in their neighbourhoods
- to enable families to use the services available to them effectively
- to tackle issues which concern us, together
- to enable models of good parenting to be shared and developed by the members.

Our Annual Reports usually contain short accounts of the work in each of the seven local Units and the Family House and also include an important section, VOICES, recording the impressions, ideas and experiences of our members. These accounts provide some evidence that our aims, which relate to the education, health and social welfare of our members, are being maintained effectively. They also provide a testimony to the dedication and commitment of the one hundred and eighty unpaid and paid people who ensure that our work goes on through their involvement in the Federation Council (the policy making and co-ordinating body), the Units and the Family House.

Since, (with the exception of statutory agency representatives on the Federation Council), every one is a member, we use the organization as a means of empowering our members to undertake responsibilities and tasks which they may not have felt within their abilities or competence when joining. Half of our paid workers, for instance, have come from the membership and have been appointed in open competition with candidates from elsewhere, many of them professionally qualified.

Our main activity centres around weekly neighbourhood groups for parents, led by convenors trained and supported from the membership. Each group has a crèche and all crèche workers receive initial and ongoing training. Unit Co-ordinators and the group convenors provide a home visiting service for members undergoing times of particular difficulty. This work is linked to short residential breaks in our Family House when members and co-ordinators feel such support is appropriate.

In common with many organizations working with families, we have found that the pressures on low income families have significantly increased over the past ten years. We are engaged in much more crisis work since the first survey of membership was conducted by Denise Hevey in 1980. A more detailed survey of the membership undertaken last year provided much data on income, health conditions and living conditions of members.

The current membership remains at about 450 families (these would be classified 'active cases' in SSD terms) and the survey showed there were 900 children most of whom attended the crèches on a weekly basis.

Much of our work focuses on helping individual parents to feel more valued and positive about themselves in a variety of roles including parenthood. It also reinforces the expert knowledge the members have about their own children. Our experience suggests that people who are confident in themselves, and in their ability to communicate with children and others, are more likely to be effective parents. The work involves a high investment of time and energy in face to face contact, but this method seems to be more likely to succeed than other approaches which do not convey any sense of belief in the parents' potential for change.

So how does our work encompass a concept of partnership? Within the neighbourhood group meetings there is a continual exchange of ideas and reinforcement about ways of bringing up children. Health issues are frequently raised, often in the context of problems arising from poor communication with and by health professionals. The majority of members have an expert knowledge of their own children's behaviours, attributes, likes and dislikes. The groups provide opportunities for members to rehearse and clarify the ways in which they may express this expertise to others, especially to professionals who are busy, and who may have limited listening skills. In this way possible power imbalances in prospective partnerships between health professionals and parents can be redressed and improved, to the benefit of the children and the families involved.

The groups are also a vehicle for exchanging information. Many field workers from housing, health, social services and educational establishments visit the groups to give information on issues which concern members and to join in subsequent discussion of points raised. Such exchanges help members to channel their subsequent requests for help more accurately, and so reduce the uneconomic use of staff time in the agencies concerned. This point was borne out in a survey of patient use of a Southampton General Practice in 1977, which showed that the reasons for attending the surgery by SCOPE members registered with it, changed from conditions related to their own state of health to specific requests for help for their children.

The process of partnership in SCOPE begins with support for members. Support involves coordinators and group convenors in understanding the family situations of members. It means offering friendship and a network of contacts; valuing the experience of members; providing opportunities for personal growth; believing in the membership; being with parents, if they so wish, at case conferences and other meeting with professionals.

Relationships with other agencies, usually through local fieldworkers, need to be maintained by the Unit co-ordinators. It is their responsibility to achieve a level of credibility with colleagues in other agencies which will engender trust in their judgement and understanding of family situations. So, the quality of partnerships with other agencies cannot be taken for granted. Such relationships are not automatic but have to be carefully nurtured by the co-ordinators. There is a significant difference, of course, between the status of staff from statutory agencies and those from a non-statutory organization such as SCOPE, arising from the legal powers of the former. Nevertheless, our experience reinforces the view that the work of both is considerably enhanced when the two groups of staff understand and value each other's roles in relation to the families within their care.

Scenarios provided for participants in the workshop on SCOPE's approach during the conference, 'Partnership and the Children Act' illustrated how, in some instances involving members, such partnerships can become tokenist and opportunities to provide well focused services for the families concerned can be missed. More importantly, in the examples given, the best interests of the children were not, in our opinion, being met by the intervening agencies.

A number of conditions are required in order to create and maintain working partnerships between non-statutory agencies such as SCOPE, which offer preventive services, and statutory agencies which maintain child protection services as part of their work with families.

- *Clarity of roles*
  Defining what each agency expects of the other in working with a family; ensuring that the family understands what these roles will be.
- *Good communication*
  Making sure that field workers in each agency keep in touch with each other and note any unexpected variations in the services a family is receiving.
- *Individual rights*
  Realisation by all involved that the rights of children will be upheld in child protection cases preferably, with the agreement of the parents. Understanding that Advocacy is likely to be used by voluntary agencies in giving support to parents.
  Recognizing that the reporting and recording systems place particular requirements on workers which vary from one organization to another.

The work of SCOPE is supported by grants from Hampshire Social Services; Hampshire Education Committee; the district health authorities of Southampton and South West Hampshire, Portsmouth and South East Hampshire, Basingstoke, and Winchester; and the City Councils of Southampton and Portsmouth. At the time of writing we are about to enter into a service agreement with Hampshire County Council for the provision of services for families. Although a service agreement formally defines the relationship between purchaser and provider, much of the local detailed work of establishing and maintaining partnerships at a local level mentioned above will still need to be undertaken.

PARTNERSHIP AND THE COMPLAINTS PROCEDURE

Based on the workshop by Gwen James
Original recording by Hazel Osborn

It has been questioned whether partnership, which implies some equality of status and power, is possible between parents and workers of statutory agencies, and between children and social workers, because the power balance is, and in some cases has to be, unequal (Holman, 1992). The mechanism which brings a measure of greater equality into the system is the power under the legislation for children and service users, in specific situations, to make a complaint.

Social workers working in local social service departments have specific duties and powers under the legislative framework which will mean that they always hold the power balance. In the extreme, social services, with the authority of the court, can remove a child permanently from their family. Under Section 17 of the Children Act, the local authority social worker has specific duties in responding to a child who may be 'in need', but how that 'need' is interpreted by the agency and how specific need is interpreted by the social worker can be open to question. In this case, the social worker has the power of resource gatekeeper. With a child who is being looked after, especially a child who is isolated from his or her family, the carer has an immense physical and psychological hold over that child, which can be used for good or ill. The power balance is further weighted in favour of local authorities, because service users are aware of these powers. When you talk to a policeman you are careful what you say.

Where there is power, there is always the possibility of the abuse of that power. There is also the reality that social workers, being human, make mistakes, or by acts of omission cause unnecessary distress. It may be too that the policies of the agency impinge unfairly on certain cases. The balance of power cannot be equal, but the balance is made more equal by the opportunity of those who feel they have been wronged in some way to make a complaint, or a 'representation' about the service they have received.

Complaints procedures also have other positive contributions. In business it is well accepted that representations from service users are a valuable method for improving the quality of the service. If people have the opportunity to say what they feel is wrong, it is possible in some cases to right that wrong, if not for them then for others.

Under the Children Act 1989:

> Every local authority shall establish a procedure for considering any representations (including any complaint) made to them by:
> a) any child who is being looked after by them, or who is not being looked after by them but is in need;
> b) a parent of his;
> c) any person who is not a parent of his but who has parental responsibility for him;
> d) any local authority foster parent;
> e) such other person as the local authority consider has a sufficient interest in the child's welfare to warrant his representations being considered by them, about the discharge by the authority of any of their functions under this Part in relation to the child.
> (Children Act 1989, section 26.3)

The Act also clearly states that at least one person who is not a member or officer of the authority should take part in the investigation of the complaint.

A Voice for the Child in Care, and in particular Gwen James, was one of the first independent agencies to offer a truly independent voice in the Representations Procedure for children and young people being looked after. VCC are now working with IRCHIN (Independent Representation for Children In Need) to provide an advice, advocacy and representation service for children in secure units. The original service was started in 1985 by people who were acting as Independent Persons on review panels for young people in secure care. They felt it was very important that young people were actually seen and their views heard. VCC now train and accredit independent representatives right across England and Wales and link them to specific secure units. VCC also run a service for all children who are being looked after.

In some senses a complaint can be seen as part of the communication process between service users and local authorities. Local authorities need to give more information about their services and their complaints procedures, complaints should be encouraged. Indeed, a recent report has suggested that where a local authority has very few complaints from children this should be regarded not as a positive sign but as a possible negative sign that young people may not know about the procedure. (Buchanan et al., 1993). Also, part of the communication process is the setting up of local support groups to elicit feedback from users, both in communities, but also in residential and other settings for young people. In this way, users have a chance to say what is wrong without making a formal representation.

Making a complaint and following this through can be a stressful event, especially for a young person. They need support in making this complaint, and they need to be sure that the person investigating the complaint is truly independent. Many young people in the above study were anxious that the person investigating the complaint was not truly independent. Young people also have an immediacy about their lives which means waiting is difficult. Independent Advocacy Services and Children's Rights Officers, who are at the end of a telephone, perform a useful function in supporting such young people.

It may be that similar supports need to be developed so that other service users feel better able to voice their grievances. We need to learn that complaints can be constructive.

8 Best partnership practice in a local authority

This chapter describes some initiatives taken by one local authority (Hampshire) in developing partnership practice under the Children Act. Hampshire is a very large and demographically diverse authority, encompassing large urban areas such as Portsmouth and Southampton, newer towns such as Andover and Basingstoke, extensive rural areas, as well as naval and military families. Contrary to the stereotype of a shire county, there are, within the area, extensive pockets of poverty and disadvantage, both in the towns and in the rural communities. The county is divided into areas, with each area having responsibility for its budget and having considerable autonomy in the way it responds to local needs and provides services. Some services such as training are co-ordinated centrally and bought in by the areas as appropriate.

The initiatives included here are described by practitioners involved in the projects. These practitioners were recommended by their authority and took part in a poster display of 'Best Partnership Practice' at the conference in Southampton 1992. They are only examples of the many innovative schemes taking place in the county. The first three schemes described were co-ordinated centrally within the county, and illustrate how the authority sets the ethos of working in partnership through training, consumer involvement, and information for service users. In the second half of the chapter, initiatives from local area, describe how teams responded to partnership issues in meeting the needs of specific groups in their communities.

INITIATIVES FROM THE CENTRE

Diana King, Jon Philpot and Vaughan Tudor Williams

Training

Training, if it is to effect working in partnership, should reflect the principles it purports to uphold. Two important partnership features of child care training in Hampshire are the inter-agency/joint-agency training and the involvement of consumers.

Winton House is the central training unit for Hampshire. At Winton House there are a group of child care trainers who provide a variety of introductory, comprehensive and specialist courses as part of the strategy for training social services staff in Hampshire. The strategy has also involved working with many other agencies to provide joint inter-agency courses, and working with the voluntary and independent sectors. The training has been based on a variety of excellent training packages from the Family Rights Group, the Open University and the National Children's Bureau. An important feature of many of these courses is that consumers are also involved.

Two inter-agency training projects, which are models of partnership work with children and families, have been running for a number of years. These are the Inter-Agency Child Protection Project and the Joint Investigation training. Over the past three years, two and a half thousand staff have received training through the Inter-Agency Child Protection Project. The second phase of the training will provide more intensive training in prevention, child protection and aftercare.

Joint-investigation work in Hampshire resulted from a pilot project in 1988 between Hampshire Social Services and Hampshire Constabulary where practitioners were both involved in joint training and joint working. The primary aim of this project was the protection and welfare of the child or young person, including the reduction of trauma and enhanced services through co-ordination, co-operation and communication between agencies. This joint training is now standard practice throughout the authority for the relevant practitioners.

Consumer involvement – The Listening to Children Project

Throughout the county, service users are involved in planning and other forums, to ensure services are responsive to their needs. One of the more innovative schemes has been an initiative focusing on partnership with young people. The long term project was launched in the Autumn of 1992 with three events for young people at venues which appealed to

97

them. The young people invited had all been looked after by Hampshire and were between the ages of 13 and 21. The purpose of the meetings was:

- *To get feedback from young people about*:
  - their experiences of being looked after
  - their needs/wants re leaving care
  - how they feel that they might best be supported by Social Services
- *This feedback was necessary to:*
  - help set standards
  - guide policy making
  - to try to ensure smooth and painless transitions for young people from being looked after to independent living
  - to live up to the spirit of the Children Act
  - to help young people to be better informed
  - to maximize the opportunities for young people to have happy and successful adult lives.

Findings from this project are being collated. It has been interesting that many of the themes highlighted by the young people from the Dolphin Project have been reinforced in this work.

Access to information

Central to the principle of partnership is that service users should have the information from which they can make informed choices. Hampshire have developed a considerable number of information booklets for service users. The following two schemes illustrate how this has been done with two groups of service users.

Guidebook for young people who are being looked after

One of their more interesting schemes is an information pack to help young people who are being looked after by Local Authority Social Services. It is designed to give young people who are being looked after all the information they need, and to which they are entitled under the provisions of the Children Act. It comes complete in a ring binder format, and is written in an attractive and accessible style. Among the areas covered by the Guidebook are:

- How the system works
- 'The Children Act' and legal terms
- Where you might live
- Education
- Health

- Leisure
- Religion/racial origin/culture /equal opportunities
- Becoming independent.

This Guidebook, which can be personalized by the local authority, is now available nationally.

Our Special Children: information for parents and carers of special children

This information book is another useful initiative for parents and carers of children with special needs. The book is a compact source of information and guidance on a wide range of available services.

PARTNERSHIP AND CHILD PROTECTION

Ruth Forrester

There are a number of important supports for good partnership practice in child protection in Hampshire. The philosophical basis of both the Children Act 1989 and the Department of Health Regulations 'Working Together' form the basis of practice. This is supported in Hampshire by very thorough training programmes for staff, as mentioned above, detailed procedures, clear quality standards, departmental values and devolved budgets. In the local area described here, these interact together to produce an ethos where vigorous participation by parents, carers, children and young people is valued and promoted. Monitoring through a very sophisticated module of the computerized client record system ensures that each part of the organization is aware of its performance and can take steps to improve it.

Although the Social Services Department has the lead role for Child Protection, it is essentially an inter-agency service and the steps to promote participation have been negotiated with the other agencies who make up the 'Core Team' – the Police, the Health Authorities, the Probation Service, the Education Service and the Armed Forces. This negotiation has occurred at the Area Child Protection Committee (the county body) and has continued at district and local (area) levels through regular meetings of core teams and joint training. This is not an easy process, as the Child Protection Service has to balance the risk to the child, against the need to promote maximum participation by parents and children.

Child protection processes

There are a large number of good practices which have developed at both the initial stage of the investigation and at Child Protection Conferences. At the initial investigation, as far as possible, parents and children are told of the reason for the investigation and their consent to interviews was obtained in writing. No investigation without parental consent, can take place without using legal procedures. Parents are involved, as far as possible, in the interviewing of children and young people, and their views are taken into account when the decision is made whether or not to hold a Child Protection Conference. Dialogue with solicitors and other advocates is also welcomed. Interpreters are provided if necessary and specialist staff are involved if the child or parent has special needs. Letters explaining the outcome of investigations are sent to parents and children. The investigation takes place within a very tight time-scale ensuring that the family is placed under stress for a limited period of time.

Child Protection Conferences

The investigating social worker is responsible for briefing the family prior to the Child Protection Conference. A leaflet prepared by the Hampshire Social Services Department is supplied, together with the Family Rights Group booklet 'Child Protection Conferences, and a letter inviting the parents and child to the Conference. Before the Conference the family meets with the Chair who explains who is attending and the main issues. Financial assistance is offered to compensate for loss of earnings. Interpreters are present if necessary. One Service Manager commented recently that it was hard to envisage an effective Child Protection Conference without family participation.

The Conference follows a pre-set Agenda which is shared with the family. Seating arrangements are carefully considered so that the family can sit next to somebody they know. Solicitors and other advocates are welcome to attend to offer support. Conferences are kept small because large Conferences are very intimidating. Parents are only excluded in exceptional circumstances, and normally parents and older children are present throughout. Families have the opportunity to question each contributor and to express their views on registration. If an inter-agency plan is agreed to help the family, their views are sought.

Outcomes are sent to families, including the Child Protection Plan which sets out causes for concern with clear expectations on everybody including the family to make changes. Children on the Child Protection Register are reviewed every three months.

Future developments

The involvement of parents and children in the joint planning of services in child protection is not yet developed. However, it is intended that future planning of services may involve genuine consultation with service users.

PARTNERSHIP AND FAMILY SUPPORT IN A RURAL AREA

Alton Family Resource Centre

The very word 'partnership' implies some sort of physical closeness. This project is of interest because it illustrates how the problem of physical distance has been overcome in providing supportive services at a Family Resource Centre for children and families who may be in need. The work of this Family Resource Team which was set up in 1991, is as diverse and varied as the area for which a service is provided. The team covers a population of approximately 83,249 spread over 160 square miles. Communities vary from small hamlets made up of a few houses and farms, to small country towns which have expanded over recent years to provide homes for young families. These young families are often cut off from the support of their extended families. The area also covers service families from both the Army and the Royal Air Force.

Hampshire Social Services have a commitment to a needs-led policy. Despite the difficulties of the wide geographical and rural nature of the area, the team aims to provide on-going support for the families, as far as possible where the needs are, that is within their own communities. The following are just two initiatives that have enabled this to happen.

One of the centre's most valuable resources is the team of Sessional Workers, who are recruited , assessed, trained and supervised by Family Resource Workers. These sessional workers come from a variety of backgrounds. They have multiple skills which extend and supplement the work undertaken by core team members. In common with all the work, an agreement is drawn up between the family and the Resource Centre outlining the method and aims to be undertaken. The involvement of a sessional worker, often from their own community, provides the support that hopefully will prevent a difficulty becoming a problem.

Support comes in a variety of forms. Recently a need for support was identified by parents in the north of the area covered. One member of the team, together with a health visitor, set up a parents' support group. Parents met in groups to share positive and negative feelings about parenthood. This provided isolated parents with a long term network. Step by step they have grown in confidence to the point where they now

101

run the group and welcome other parents who feel the need of support and friendship.

The role of the Family Resource Team in interpreting the needs of the families and the area it serves, is constantly developing. Central to this is the commitment to working in partnership with colleagues from other agencies, both voluntary and statutory to provide the service as identified by users.

PARTNERSHIP IN A LOCALLY BASED CHILDREN'S HOME

Jackie Walton

In this project, partnership is seen as both working with individuals, families and significant others, as well as working in partnership with colleagues. The shared common goal of the project is to enable young people to live with their own families, failing that with alternative families, and/or independently. But, as far as possible, the young people are maintained in their community. In this project, working in partnership with colleagues is essential to working successfully in partnership with families.

Residential care has to be seen as a positive part of a care package. Therefore the locally-based children's home is part of an integrated child care service which includes the area office, family resource centre and child-guidance.

The locally-based children's home for Eastleigh has adopted various approaches to the care of children, to prevent them spending a large proportion of their childhood growing up in residential care. Some of these approaches are:

- Time-limited planned placements as a part of a care package are offered with a view to rehabilitation back into the community.
- Where possible only 5-day care is offered, with young people returning to their families at weekends and for extended periods during school holidays. This maintains links with the family and community.
- Parents retain parental responsibility and they are encouraged to continue to provide the young person with basic requirements such as pocket money and clothing.
- The home provides the opportunity for a young person to maintain links within the community by encouraging young people to continue to use the services of their local community such as schools, doctors, dentists, Department of Social Security, and other services.
- Staff in the home are able to build good links and lines of communication with community services to enable them to work with young people and families.

The primary role of the residential unit is to offer residential care, however, the unit can offer other services:

- Out of hours support
- Outreach work
- Holiday activities
- Family assessment
- Daycare/group work
- Case holding/keywork
- Respite care
- Supportive lodgings/post 16 support.

The above work can only be undertaken because of the quality and experience of the residential staff team. One third of the team is qualified, one third is currently undertaking professional qualification training, whilst others have considerable experience and/or qualifications in related fields. Training is given high priority in the unit with all staff expected to undertake on-going training which includes Children Act awareness, race awareness, equal opportunities, as well as practice issues. All staff undergo an annual appraisal to assess training needs.

The role of this residential unit continues to evolve and change to meet the changing needs of the community. In planning future services it has been important to listen to the views of service users and actively seek their views.

PARTNERSHIP AND A FAMILY LINK SCHEME FOR FAMILIES WITH SPECIAL NEEDS

Jan Goodwin

This project aims to support families who have a child with disabilities. The Family Link Scheme is an excellent example of multi-agency partnership. Funding is through the Joint Planning initiative and moneys come from The Health Authority, Social Services, The Spastics Society and Mencap. Coordinators work closely with a variety of agencies. The role of the scheme is to act as the enabler to families so that they can develop their own supportive partnership relationships. This is done by:

- Providing local flexible family based respite care for children with disabilities
- Providing the child who has disabilities with an opportunity to make friends and widen his/her social circle.

103

There are 14 Family Link Schemes in operation throughout Hampshire. In order to provide such a service the role of the co-ordinator is to:

- Recruit, assess, train and support carers
- Assess the needs of the family and child
- Match and introduce carers and user families
- Support the link.

Parents are enabled to take control of their link and frequently make their own arrangements. The role of the co-ordinator in the first instance is to ensure that all necessary approval procedures are followed. All carers attend a six session training course run by the co-ordinator. This involves parents and experienced carers. Specialist training in handling is usually given by the parents (they know best) and experts from the Health Service and Schools are always available.

After an initial introduction period is completed, an agreement is reached between the two families and a plan of support made. This plan can be as flexible as necessary to suit the needs of the child and his/her family.

PARTNERSHIP AT A RESOURCE CENTRE FOR CHILDREN WHO HAVE SPECIAL NEEDS

Gill Farmer and Jill Blanchard

This project illustrates the practicalities of working in partnership with families at a resource centre with children who have special needs. In this setting, partnership relationship are made with the families, as well as with other agencies. In addition an important role is helping families themselves to develop their own multi-agency partnerships with other professionals.

The Nursery based at Eastleigh Family Resource Centre was established in October 1990 to provide a service to children who have special needs and their families, and who live in the Borough of Eastleigh. The Nursery is funded by the Health, Education and Social Services Departments. There is a commitment to working in partnership with parents to help children fulfil their potential and, where possible, eventually integrate them into mainstream playgroup or education provisions.

The Nursery provides a service to children aged 0-5, parents and siblings. The criteria for places being offered are:

- Children who have disabilities
- Children who have a significant developmental delay/speech disorder etc.

- Children and parents who have relationship difficulties, or where there are control or child protection issues.

Referrals are made by a variety of representatives from the three funding agencies. There is a monthly panel meeting which considers referrals and the allocation of Nursery places. Panel members include; the Family Resource Centre Manager; Nursery Teacher; Nursery Leader; Health Visitor; Head Teacher of the local Special School and an Educational Psychologist.

Prior to a request for a place being considered, an initial assessment interview will have been undertaken and the parent and child will have visited the Nursery. Every child has a key worker. Work programmes are developed reflecting the child's needs and the parent's wishes.

We aim to offer children who have disabilities or significant developmental delays, a minimum of two three hour sessions a week. A developmental assessment will be completed by the Nursery Teacher when the child has attended for six weeks. There are three-monthly reviews involving the Nursery Teacher, parents, keyworker and therapists.

The staff complement consists of a Nursery Leader who has responsibility for processing referrals and undertakes individual and group work with parents, a Nursery Teacher who has primary responsibility for child assessments, work programmes, staff supervision, reviews and evaluation, and three part-time nursery nurses who implement individual programmes, make home visits and undertake some outreach work to playgroups.

The Nursery provides:

- A team of experienced, professionally-qualified nursery staff who have specific skills in working with children who have special needs
- Regular pre-planned occupational, speech and physiotherapist input available on site
- Regular visits from a Paediatric Consultant
- Access to Child Psychiatrist
- Access to Clinical Psychologist
- Access to Educational Psychologist assessment
- Parent support groups
- Opportunities for play and personal development in a safe and stimulating environment and a chance to explore all types of mediums
- Access to counselling services to address specific problems
- High Staff ratios.

CONCLUSION

This chapter highlights some necessary components in partnership practice. Firstly, although budgets may be devolved to areas, the authority sets the ethos for practice through its policy, strategies, quality standards, procedures, training, and information for consumers. The areas then have to look to the needs of their service users, and develop services which are responsive to those needs. Each area will have different demographic and geographical issues to confront. Service users, who should be involved in planning forums, will come up with different priorities. There can be no prescriptive answer as to how services should be provided. Innovation may be King and Queen.

Working in partnership takes on many meanings. All services should be endeavouring to work in partnership with families, but it is equally important to work with children, young people and significant others. In order to do this, agency workers will have to work in partnership with their colleagues, other professionals and also with other agencies. Working in partnership may also mean acting as a facilitator for parents to work in partnership supporting each other, as well as facilitating parents to make relationships with other professionals.

Finally, a recurring theme from these initiatives, is that you cannot stand still. Processes have to be in place which ensure services can continue to adapt and develop. Needs are constantly changing. Working in partnership means agencies need to keep listening, keep interpreting and keep responding.

Part Four
CONCLUSIONS

9 Partnership: future issues

Ann Buchanan

The child's welfare shall be the court's paramount consideration
(Children Act 1989, section 1)

It shall be the duty of every local authority...
(a) to safeguard and promote the welfare of children within their area who are in need; and
(b) so far as is consistent with that duty to promote the upbringing of such children by their families
(Children Act 1989, section 17)

In this last chapter we return to basics. This chapter is about reminding ourselves what we are trying to achieve and looking at some of the mechanisms which may help or hinder this process.

We need to remember that 'partnership' is not an end objective. Working in partnership is merely a vehicle which may facilitate the above obligations to children being met. Although there is substantive evidence that partnership can be effective in supporting children and families in need, protecting children as well as keeping them with and returning them to their families (Gibbons, 1992), there is a danger that 'working in partnership' will become in itself another unquestioned ideology which as long as you are doing it, you can assume all is well.

Partnership has become a buzz word of the 1990s.
This nice-sounding term makes us feel good, perhaps even to the extent of being offered as a solution to all child-care difficulties.
(Family Rights Group, 1991)

Monitoring and evaluation

The challenge for the 1990s is to ensure the Act is indeed achieving what it set out to do, and that working in partnership is facilitating this process. Partnership is not the only buzz word of our times. There is a concern for 'Quality', 'Standards' and 'Audits', 'Accountability'. Many local authorities, as well as collecting data for the Department of Health, are now developing their own schemes for monitoring and evaluating the Children Act.

In Hampshire, monitoring is seen as a day to day statistical activity. The main mechanism for monitoring is the client record system (CRS), which is updated and computerized daily, and from which reports on data and subsequent statistics can be created. They are soon to pilot a new Assessment and Care Management System which will include considerable extra data including budget monitoring and control.

Evaluation in Hampshire is seen as a longer term process and seeks to ascertain how far the aims and objectives of the Act have been achieved, and how far the required process of change has been implemented. It is an assessment against objectives, and an analysis of whether the availability of resources and the required changes are or are not on course. Included in this process would be an evaluation of the philosophy and culture, policy and practice, the procedures including multi-agency work, and the outcomes including complaints and measures of satisfaction. Evaluation would include both quantitative and qualitative data.

The first challenge is to ensure that the things that are monitored are indeed the right things. The most usual way is to identify a range of indicators that suggest that objectives are being met, and to monitor these indicators. For example, a local authority may want to monitor how well its staff are working in partnership. To do this they may count up the numbers of parents who come to child protection conferences, or the numbers of young people who attend their reviews. This may tell them about partnership practice, but it does not tell them how well children are being protected. A local authority may feel progress has been made because the numbers of young people being looked after has dropped, but that does not measure the numbers who returned home to be re-abused, or who have left care ill-prepared. It is important to ensure there are a range of indicators.

If we really want to know what is happening under the Children Act 1989, monitoring based on number counts is not enough. Statistics may not lie but they do not tell the whole truth. Local authorities need to invest in evaluation processes which include both quantitative and qualitative data. Talking to users does not give the whole picture, but it will certainly make more sense of any numbers collected. And if you want to know what to measure in the first place, there is no substitute for talking to consumers. In some authorities users are now well involved

110

in planning forums and could also be used to give an annual review of services. The conference on which this book is based is another example of bringing all the partners together on neutral territory to facilitate a sharing of experiences and ideas. Questionnaires to service users can also be helpful. In evaluation studies, we are learning that different types of responses are elicited from users by different kinds of approaches (Buchanan et al., 1993). A range of approaches is therefore indicated. At the extreme end, as we have mentioned in chapter seven, is the very positive value of a complaints procedure. But that is the end of the road. We need to make it easier for users to give feedback.

Staying afloat in a sea of paperwork

The second challenge in monitoring and reviewing is how to limit the paper work. Herbert Geering (1992), speaking of the care management approach in the USA warned the British audience that in implementing the Care in the Community proposals they risked drowning under a sea of paper work. Child care students on our MSc Diploma in Social Work course are already complaining that the long forms they have to complete in order to access services 'get in the way' of effective communication with users. Such forms may be more complicated than necessary for the specific task because, as we have seen, they have to do the double duty of giving managers information for monitoring purposes .

Individual PCs for practitioners and hand held computers are making important inroads in limiting paper work. In some cases, user records and assessments are recorded directly onto the computer. Computers demand not only technical skills but new interpersonal skills. Paradoxically it may be easier to work in partnership with families with a laptop. At least everything is open, the grounds for the assessment clear, and the options specified, whereas with a notepad the data goes back to the secrecy of the office to be written up and interpreted.

Quality bottom up not inspection down

The third challenge is to develop monitoring and evaluation systems that go up as well as down. The Social Services Inspectorate has a core task to inspect social services provided by local authorities and other agencies, in order to promote good standards of service, management and the use of resources. They also carry out a national programme of inspections to evaluate how agencies are implementing national policies and to aid development and review. In their latest report they give their commitment to:

assisting others to achieve the highest standards of provision of services for individual users and their carers in ways which make the best use of the resources of the community. We seek to work in partnership with health services and the Personal Social Services statutory, voluntary and private agencies.

(SSI, 1992)

Inspection should be a two-way process, both top-down and bottom-up. All those taking part in the inspection processes have a vehicle by which they can contribute to professional social work knowledge through the Social Services Inspectorate, who inform ministers and policy making bodies. Unfortunately, ideas from the working partners at the base place may be inhibited by the concept of inspection. Residential workers, in particular, have had difficulty in owning some of the procedures that have come top down (Buchanan et al., 1993).

In recent years the language of Quality Assurance such as 'setting standards' and 'concern for quality' has been infiltrating the reports of the Social Service Inspectorate. The term 'Quality Assurance', with its focus on the positive, has a marked psychological advantage over the term 'inspection'. Lady Wagner in a recent publication (Kahan, 1993) highlights the possible benefits of the British Standard 5750. She presented a Quality Assurance registration certificate to Napier House in Newcastle-upon-Tyne who had registered under BS5750; the national, European and international standard for quality systems.

The advantage of BS5750 is that every member of an organization, every day is involved in achieving the standard. It is real partnership in action. It is not a question of 'getting things together before the inspectors arrive'. It is a logical system for assuring quality. The essential elements are:

- A defined mission for the whole organization and a defined purpose for the individual unit
- A defined process for achieving the requirements
- A defined system for monitoring and recording success or failure
- A defined system for monitoring the record
- A defined system for auditing the system
- A defined process for corrective action if the quality system has failed
- A defined system for reviewing the requirements and procedures
- A defined process for reviewing the whole system

(Kahan, 1993)

BS5750 presents a number of problems in its adaptation to child care settings. It has been argued that there is no place for such measures in child care, in that the needs of children are so diverse, and standards

112

within a home could be completely blown apart by one particularly challenging young person. But BS5750 is about procedures which should be followed. These should reflect good child care practice. They have to be written showing exactly what needs to be assessed. A Procedures Manual is then produced which is a specific statement of how the system operates, as well as a Quality Manual which outlines the quality management system. One or two members of staff are then trained as auditors and carry out internal audits to see the standard is maintained. The whole system is then assessed by independent assessors. Independent assessors would talk to the children and young people as part of quality assurance.

It has also been argued that registration and audit is expensive. Originally it was felt that each individual establishment would have to register, but local authorities can now register all their establishments, or groups of establishments as one unit. As a number of private homes for the elderly are now registered, it must be considered financially viable. A possible disadvantage would be that if one establishment fell below standard all the others would loose their award, but this could encourage all homes to keep up standards.

The ideas from BS5750 of involving all partners, not just the professional ones, in setting the standards, monitoring the quality, and having national recognition for the efforts made by all in achieving that quality, is attractive and is worthy of further consideration.

The split taking place between purchaser and provider in child care services in many authorities is moving practice in this direction. As provider units become responsible for their own finances and have to compete on the open market, they are having to define the services they provide and the systems they have in place to ensure quality. In the future, in order to attract purchasers, they may want to make the short additional leap into nationally recognized systems of Quality Assurance. One privately run children's home with education is already registered.

assessment .

The search for national standards in child care

Nationally recognized standards in child care may not be so far off. Within the next two years the Department of Health is hoping to introduce mandatory Assessment and Action Records which should be kept on all children who are looked after. These records, which have been developed by the Dartington Research Team over the last five years as part of the Looking After Children project offer a number of exciting possibilities. Basically they are a working tool to ensure that vital aspects in the lives of children and young people who are being looked after are assessed and monitored at regular intervals. They are so designed that necessary steps have to be taken to follow up any identified needs. The forms provide an ongoing record on a specific child which can be used for a number of purposes in planning that child's care. They could even be used as part of the standards procedures in a BS5750. The records can then be computerized, giving vital information to local authorities managers and, furthermore data which can be passed on to the Department of Health to give the first national data of young people being looked after. The assessment records are being tested at present. A group of children and young people who are not being looked after are also involved in the testing programme. This will give a valuable comparative baseline on children living in the community. A number of international bodies have also shown an interest in adapting the records for their services, which offers the possibility of trans-cultural research.

Assessment and action records, by listing questions that have to be answered, are the first national attempt to define national standards. There have been considerable difficulties in undertaking this project. One of the difficulties is that in setting standards, they are defining what is 'good enough parenting'. The dilemma is that 'good enough parenting' and quality child care are moving phenomena that change over time and between cultures. The danger about setting very precise standards is that they might freeze child welfare services at a moment in time. However, the benefits of the system would appear to far outweigh any disadvantages.(Parker et al., 1991: *Looking After Children: Assessment and Action Records*)

Keeping the information flowing

Nearly two years after the implementation of the Children Act 1989, there is some excitement that the Act may be achieving at least some of its aims. (DOH, 1992: Children Act Report) The Department of Health and the Social Service Inspectorate have made impressive efforts to disseminate information in the last two years . The SSI alone have published over 180 separate items. More than 100 of these relate to child care. Even so, dissemination of information is still a problem. One of the problems is that some of the documents are written in language which fails to communicate to those who need to be informed, for example some of the leaflets to young people. Another problem is that accessing the relevant material can be difficult. Dare I say, as a specialist in this area, and someone who has had a responsibility for passing this information onto over 100 potential social work practitioners a year, that I am fairly certain I have not seen all the documents.

Professor Michael Peckham in a recent report from the Department of Health 'Research for Health', discusses how information needs to be transferred systematically to the point of use and entered into practice through the appropriate information vehicle (Peckham, 1993). We used to think that information, particularly research information, was the prerogative of the professional. Working in partnership questions this assumption. It may be that the best dissemination vehicle is the engine of the people, and that more information about services and innovative ideas from other parts of the country should be deliberately focused towards the public through newspapers, radio, television and videos. It is happening already, but greater public relations expertise is needed to keep the engine on the railroad and to avoid some of the sensationalism. In medicine there is the interesting role reversal that the public by demanding a service, may be forcing the general practitioner to learn about that service.

Planning for change

We cannot stand still. Hopefully new knowledge demonstrates better ways to do things. Systems, although bursting at the seams under the joint pressures of time and lack of resources, still need to be flexible and responsive to change. The following story makes an appropriate finale to this book. It illustrates how one hard pressed social worker in a local children and families team with, no doubt, dozens of priority child care cases, was able to stand back and find the time and energy to implement an idea he had read about. It illustrates how the management structure within which he worked was responsive to change and was able to give him necessary support to implement his idea.

The local field social worker in question rang me to ask if I would be prepared to train as a Group Co-ordinator in a pilot project on Family Group Conferences. This is an interesting development from New Zealand whereby social workers have been able to reduce what they call 'stranger placements' of children and young people by more than 60% and up to as much as 90% in some areas (Wilcox et al., 1991). The idea is that family members (this would include extended family and even significant people with whom the family may not actually be related) of a child who has been at risk of significant harm or other child protection issues, are brought together by an independent (of social services) co-ordinator, and then allowed to deliberate in private and decide on a plan for care and protection of that child. The role of the professional agencies is to produce assessment information for conferences and help facilitate and review the family's plan after the conference.

Under this scheme in New Zealand, the initial child protection referral is met with the same response as in this country. There is an emphasis on agreed procedures, co-working and multi-agency work. The child's interests always remain paramount. However, key differences emerge following this initial contact. Two clearly separate roles are identified. The first requires the investigating social worker to make assessments in conjunction with other agencies and produce this information in full for the Family Group Conference to consult. The second role requires a separate Care and Protection Co-ordinator to convene the Family Group Conference. The Co-ordinator will identify and map-out family and extended family and ensure they are enabled to attend the conference. A great deal of preparatory work is undertaken by the co-ordinator who consults with the Family Group regarding date, time and venue of the conference. The family only have to answer two questions:

1) Is this child in need of care and protection?
2) If so, what is your plan for the child?

The family can call back the professionals at any time to clarify points or take advice on resources available. If the plan is agreed the family is helped to implement their plan by various agencies.

To date, three local authorities in the UK have shown interest in Family Group Conferences, and the Family Rights Group have established a support consultancy group for any agencies interested. An important impetus for the approach in New Zealand is, as in the UK, that state provision can provide no guarantee of safety for children.

The principles behind the family group conferences are set out in guidelines by the Department of Social Welfare in New Zealand.

> Rather than using the power of the department alone to confront and change a pattern of abuse, power also comes from the presence of extended family. The process requires families to take up their responsibilities and workers to shed some of their power. Responsibility for the ongoing well-being of the child is taken up by those with life-long ties to that child.
>
> (Wilcox et al., 1991)

I was just finishing this book when I learnt about Family Group Conferences. I find them an exciting new concept which, if they worked, could change the structure of child welfare. This sums up the message from this book. Working in partnership under the Children Act is not something that happened on October 14, 1991. Working in partnership under the Children Act is one of the processes which help implement the aims of the Act, and what it means is evolving daily in practice.

So now at the end of this book what does working in partnership under the Children Act mean? I thought I knew last week, but maybe now you need to ask me next year.

References

Aldgate, J. (1989), *Using Written Agreements with Children and Families,*. Family Rights Group, London.

American Association Protecting Children (1986), *Highlights of Official Child Neglect and Abuse Reporting*, AAPC.

Baird, C. (ed.) (1988), *Development of Risk Assessment Indices for Alaskan Family Services*, National Council Crime Delinquency, Madison Wisconsin.

Berrios G.E. & Mohanna M. (1990), 'Durkheim and French psychiatric views on suicide during the 19th century', *British Journal of Psychiatry*, 156 1-9

Beeforth, M., Conlon, E., Field, V., Hoser, B., Sayce, L. (eds.) (1990), *Whose service is it anyway? User's Views on Co-ordinating Community Care*, Research and Development for Psychiatry.

Bodmer, Sir Walter (1988), 'New Approaches to the Prevention and Treatment of Cancer' in Austyn J.M. (ed.) *New Prospects for Medicine*, Oxford University Press, Oxford.

Bourget, D. & Bradford, J.M.W. (1990), 'Homicidal parents', *Canadian Journal of Psychiatry*, 35 3 233-238.

Buchanan, A. (1992), *Interim Report on The Dolphin Project, Views of Young People on The Children Act 1989*, Department of Social Work Studies, University of Southampton.

Buchanan, A., Wheal, A., Walder, D., Macdonald, S., Coker, R. (1993), *Answering Back, Report of young people being looked after on the Children Act 1989*, CEDR, Department of Social Work Studies, University of Southampton.

117

Burch, G. & Mohr, V. (1980), 'Evaluating a child abuse intervention programme', *Social Casework* 61.2 90-99.

Burns, L. (1991), *Partnership with Families: A Study of 65 Child Protection Conferences in Gloucestershire to which the Family were invited*, Gloucester Social Services Department, Gloucester.

Butler Sloss, E. (1988), *Report of the Inquiry into Child Abuse in Cleveland 1987*, Cmnd 412 HMSO.

Calami, R. & Franchi, C. (1987), *Child Abuse and its Consequences: Observational Approaches*, Cambridge Univ Press, Cambridge.

Commission for Racial Equality (1991), *From Cradle to School: a practical guide to race equality and childcare*, Commission for Racial Equality

Concise Oxford Dictionary (1975), Oxford University Press.

Creighton, S. (1993), 'Child murder statistics as an indicator of effective protection – a reply', *British Journal of Social Work* in press.

Davies, C. & Stratton, P. (eds.) (1988), *Early Prediction and Prevention of Child Abuse*, 43-57 Wiley, Chichester.

De'Ath, E. & Pugh, G. (eds.) (1985-6), *Partnership Papers*, National Children's Bureau.

Department of Health (1982), *Child Abuse – A study of Inquiry Reports 1973-1981*, HMSO.

Department of Health (1986) *Child Abuse – Working Together. A draft guide for arrangements for inter-agency co-operation for the protection of children*, HMSO.

Department of Health (1989), *The Care of Children: Principles and Practice in Regulations and Guidance* , HMSO.

Department of Health (1991), *Children Act 1989, Guidance and Regulations*, vol. 2, HMSO.

Department of Health (1991), *Children Act 1989, Guidance and Regulations*, vol. 3, HMSO.

Department of Health (1991), *Children Act 1989, Guidance and Regulations*, vol. 4, HMSO.

Department of Health (1991), *Children Act 1989, Guidance and Regulations*, vol. 6, HMSO.

Department of Health (1991), *Working Together, under the Children Act 1989, A Guide to arrangements for inter-agency cooperation for the protection of children from abuse*, HMSO.

Department of Health (1991), *Child Abuse – a Study of Inquiry Reports 1980-1989*, HMSO.

Department of Health (1991), *The Children Act 1989: an Introductory guide for the NHS*, HMSO.

Department of Health (1992), *Children Act Report*, HMSO.

Department of Health and Social Security (1966), *The Child, The Family and the Young Offender*, Cmd 2742, HMSO.

Department of Health and Social Security (1985), *Review of Child Care Law*, HMSO.

D'Orban, P.T. (1979), 'Women who kill their children', *British Journal of Psychiatry*, 134 560-571.

Durkheim, E . (1952), *Suicide*, Routledge Kegan Paul, London.

Elfer, P. & Gatiss, S. (1990), *Charting Child Health Services*, National Children's Bureau.

Egeland, B., Jacobwitz, D. & Papatola, K. (1987), 'Inter-generational continuity of parental abuse' in Lancaster, J. & Gelles, R. (eds.), *Bio-social aspects of Child Abuse*, Jossey-Bass, New York.

Egeland, B. (1988), 'Breaking the Cycle of Abuse' in Browne et al., op. cit., 86-99.

Finkel, K.C., (1987), 'Sexual abuse in children: An update' *Canadian Medical Association*, 136 245-252.

Family Rights Group (1991), *The Children Act 1989: Working in Partnership with Families*, HMSO.

Fitzpatrick, R., (1989), 'Gay mens' sexual behaviour in response to AIDS', in Aggleton, P. (ed.) *AIDS – Social Representations and Social Practice*, 127-146, Falmer Press, Bristol.

Franklin, B. & Parton, N. (1991), *Social Work, the Media and the General Public*, Routledge, London.

Garabino, J. (1986), 'Can we measure success in preventing child abuse?' *Child Abuse Neglect*, 10 5-15.

Geering , H. (1992), 'Care Management' – *keynote address at Community Care in New World. Boston USA*, organized by Community Care, London.

Gelles, R.J. & Edfeldt, A.W. (1986), 'Violence towards children in the United States and Sweden' *Child Abuse Neglect*, 10 4 501-510.

Gelles, R.J. (1989), 'Child abuse and violence in single-parent families: parent absence and economic deprivation', *American Journal of Orthopsychiatry*, 59.4 492-501.

Gibbons, J. (1992), *The Children Act 1989 and Family Support: Principles into Practice.*, HMSO.

Gillick v. *West Norfolk and Wisbech Area Health Authority* ,1986: AC112.

Goetting, A. (1990), 'Child victims of homicide: a portrait of their killers and the circumstances of their deaths', *Violence Victims* 5 4 287-296.

Hall, D. (ed.) (1989), *Health for all Children. A programme for child health surveillance*, Oxford University Press.

Hampshire County Council (1991), *Hampshire's Child Care Strategy*, Hampshire Social Services.

Hampshire County Council (1993), *Children First: Principles, policy and strategy*, Hampshire County Council.

Hampshire County Council (1991), *My Guidebook*, Ashford Press.

Hayden, C. (1992), *The Children Act 1989: Day Care and Supervised Activities for Under Eights. SSRIU Occasional Paper No. 24*, University of Portsmouth.

Hayden, C. (1993), *Under Eights Teams as a Mechanism for Service Delivery*, SSRIU *Occasional Paper No. 28*, University of Portsmouth.

Herrenkohl, E.C. & Herrenkohl, M. (1983), 'Circumstances surrounding the occurrence of child maltreatment', *Journal of Consulting Clinical Psychology* 51.3 424-431.

Hinchcliffe, S.A., Howard, C.V., Lynch, M.R.J. & Sargent, P.H. (1993), 'Renal developmental arrest in Sudden Infant Death Syndrome', *Paediatric Pathology*, 13 333-343.

Holman, B. (1992), 'Flaws in Partnership', *Community Care*, 20 February, 15-16.

Kahan, B. (1993), *Residential Care for Children: Report of a Department of Heath Seminar held on 30 October – 1 November 1991 at Dartington Hall Devon*. Department of Health, HMSO.

Kempe, H.C., Silverman, F.N., Steele, B.F., Droegemuller, W. & Silver, H.K. (1962), 'The Battered Child Syndrome', *Journal of American Medical Association* , 181 17-22.

Kempe, H. & Helfer, R.E. (1981), *The Battered Child*, 3rd ed., Chicago University Press, Chicago.

Krugman, R.D., Lenherr, M., Betz, L. & Fryer, G.E. (1986), 'The relationship between unemployment and physical neglect of children', *Child Abuse Neglect*, 10 3 415-418.

Lane, J., (1991), *The 1989 Children Act Framework for Racial Equality in Children's Day Care/Education*, Centre for Racial Equality.

Little, M.L. & Gibbons, J. (1992), 'Predicting the rate of children on the Child Protection Register', *Research Policy Planning* , 10 2 15-18.

Lowe, N., Murch, M., Borkowski, M., Copner, R., Griew, K. (1991), *The Use and Practice of Freeing for Adoption Provisions*, Socio-legal Centre for Family Studies, Bristol.

Luckham, S. and Golding, K. (1989), *An Analysis of Essex Social Services Child Abuse Register*, Essex County Council, Essex.

Lynch, M.J. (1988), 'The Consequences of Child Abuse' in Browne, K. et al., op. cit. 203-212.

McFate, K., Lawson, R. & Wilson, W.J. (1991), *Poverty, Inequality and the Crisis of Social Policy*, Joint Centre for Political Economic Studies, Washington DC.

McLoyd, V. (1990), 'The impact of economic hardship on black families and children: psychological distress, parenting and socio-emotional development', *Child Development*, 61 2 311-346.

Madge, N. (1983), 'Unemployment and its effect upon children', *Journal of Child Psychology Psychiatry*, 24 2 311-320.

Mackay, Lord (1988), *Presenting the Children Bill to the House of Lords*, Hansard.

Millham, S., Bullock, R.. Hosie, K. & Little, M. (1986), *Lost in Care: the Problems of Maintaining Links between Children in Care and their Families*, Gower.

Millham, et al. (1989), *Access Disputes in Child Care*, Gower.

National Health Service and Community Care Act (1990), HMSO.

Nixon, P. (1992), *Family Group Conferences, A radical approach to planning the care and protection of children*, Hampshire County Council.

Newlands, M. & Emery, J.S. (1991), 'Child abuse and cot deaths', *Child Abuse Neglect*, 15 3 275-278.

Oates, R.K. (1984), 'Persistent characteristics of parents of battered children', *Medical Journal Australia*, 140.6. 325-329.

Oliver, J.E. (1988), 'Successive generations of child maltreatment', *British Journalof Psychiatry*, 153 543-553.

Packman, J., Randall J. & Jacques, N. (1986), *Who Needs Care*, Blackwell.

Parker, J. & Asher, S. (1987), 'Peer relations and later personal adjustment: are low accepted children at risk?' *Psychological Bulletin*, 102, 357-389.

Parker, R., Ward, H., Jackson, S., Aldgate. J., Wedge, P. (1991), *Looking after Children: assessing outcomes in child care*, HMSO.

Peckham, M. (1993), *Department of Health: Research for Health*, HMSO.

Platt, S. (1984), 'Unemployment and suicidal behaviour: a review', *Social Science Medicine*, 19 85-89.

Powell, J., Marks, E., and Lovelock, R. (1992), *Child Protection Committees: an initial evaluation in Hampshire*, CEDR, Department of Social Work Studies, University of Southampton, Southampton.

Prins, H.A. (1986), *Dangerous Behaviour,the Law and Mental Disorder*, Tavistock, London.

Prins, H.A. (1988), 'Dangerous clients: further observations on the limitation of mayhem', *British Journal of Social Work*, 18 6 593-610.

Pritchard, C., Cotton, A. & Cox, M. (1990), 'Analysis of young adult clients in probation & social service caseloads: a focus upon illegal drugs and HIV infection', *Research Policy Planning*, 8 2 1-8.

Pritchard, C. (1991), 'Levels of risk and psycho-social problems of families on the "At Risk of Abuse" register: indicators of outcome two years after case closure', *Research Policy & Planning*, 9 2 19-26.

Pritchard, C. (1992a), 'Changes in elderly suicide in the USA and the developed world 1974-1987: a comparison with current homicide', *International Journal of Geriatric Psychiatry*, 7 125-134.

Pritchard, C. (1992b), 'Children's homicide as an indicator of effective child protection', *British Journal of Social Work*, 22 6 663-684.

Pritchard, C. (1992c), 'Youth suicide in Australia and New Zealand: an international comparative study', *Australian New Zealand Journal of Psychiatry*, 26 4 609-617.

Pritchard, C. (1992d), 'Is there a link between youth suicide and unemployment in England and Wales and Scotland 1973-1988? a comparison with Western Europe, *British Journal of Psychiatry*, 160 750-756.

Pritchard, C. (1992e), 'What can we afford for the N.H.S.? An analysis of Government expenditure 1964-1992, *Social Administration Policy*, 2 6 1 40-54.

Pritchard, C., Cotton, A., Godson, J. & Cox, M. (1993), 'Mental illness, drug and alcohol misuse and HIV risk behaviour in 214 young adult probation clients', *Social Work Social Science Review*, 3 3 227-242.

Pritchard. C. & Hayes, P. (1993), '*La mort subite des nourissons*', *Medicine Infantile* in press.

Pritchard, C. (1993a), 'Attempts to explain changing elderly suicide rates in the USA', *International Journal of Geriatric Psychiatry*, 8 5 437-440.

Pritchard, C. (1993b), 'Kindestotungen: Die extremste Form der Kindesmisshandlung: Ein Internationaler Vergleich zwichen Baby-Klein-kind- und Kindestotungen', *Nachrichten Dienst*, 72 3 65-72.

Pritchard, C. (1993c), 'A reply to Creighton on child murder rates in Britain and Europe', *British Journal of Social Work* , December in press.

Pritchard, C. (1993d), 'Sudden Infant Death Syndrome: evidence of a Western 'pandemic': Baby mortalities 1970-1991', in preparation.

Pugh, G. & De'Ath, E. (1985), *The needs of parents*, Macmillan Education.

Pugh, G., Aplin, G., De'Ath, E., Moxon, M. (1987), *Partnership in Action. Working with parents in pre-school centre*, National Children's Bureau.

Pugh, G. & De'Ath, E. (1989), *Working towards Partnership in the Early Years*, National Children's Bureau.

Resnick, P.J. (1980), 'Murder of the newborn: a psychiatric review of neonaticide' in Williams, G.J. & Money, J. (ed.) *Traumatic Abuse and Neglect of Children at Home*, John Hopkins University Press, 143-153, New York.

Regina v. *Tower Hamlets, LBC ex parte Byas, CA.*, 1992.

Regina v.*North Avon DC, ex parte Smith, CA.*, 1993

Roberts, J. (1988), 'Why are some families more vulnerable to abuse?' in Browne, K.,op. cit.

Rotherum-Borus, M.J. (1989), 'Evaluation of suicide risk in community settings', *Suicide Life Threatening Behaviour*, 19 1 108-119.

Rose, S.M. (1991), 'Acknowledging the abuse background of intensive case management clients', *Community Mental Health Journal*, 27 4 255-264.

Rowe, J., Cain, H., Hundleby, M. & Keane, A. (1984), *Long Term Foster Care*, Batsford/BAAF.

Rowe, J. (ed.) (1985), *Decisions in Child Care*, D.H.S.S.

Rowe, J., Hundleby M. & Garnett L. (1989), *Child Care Now* , BAAF.

Rutter, M. (1992), 'Services for children with emotional disorders: needs, accomplishments and future developments, *Young Minds. Newsletter*, No.9, 1-5.

Schaffer, M.R., Sobieraj, K., & Hollyfield, R.L. (1988), 'Prevalence of childhood physical abuse in adult male alcoholics', *Child Abuse Neglect*, 12 2 141-150.

Scott, P.D. (1973), 'Fatal battered baby cases', *Medicine Science Law*, 13 3 197-206.

Sheldon, B. (1988), 'Childhood sexual abuse in adult female psychotherapy referrals: incidence and implications for treatment', *British Journal of Psychiatry,* 152 107-111.

Somander, L.H.K. & Rammer, L.M. (1991), 'Intra-and-extra familial child homicide in Sweden 1971-1980', *Child Abuse Neglect,* 15 1-2 45-55.

Steinberg, L., Catalano, R. & Dooley, D. (1981), 'Economic antecedents of child abuse and neglect', *Child Development,* 152 107-111.

The Children Act 1989, HMSO.

Social Service Inspectorate (1992), *Concern for Quality: The First Annual Report of the Chief Inspector Social Services Inspectorate 1991/1992,* HMSO.

Stubbs, P. (1991), 'The Children Act 1989: an anti-racist perspective', *Practice 5 (3),* pp. 226-229.

Swarup, N. (1992), *Equal Voice,* SSRIU *Report No. 22.,* University of Portsmouth.

Swarup, N. (1993), *Stage II. Submission to CCETSW for the approval of a consortium of agencies as a practice learning centre for training social workers (work involved developmental work on equal opportunities issues),* University of Portsmouth.

Tunstill, J. (1992), 'Local authority policies on children in need' in Gibbons, J., *The Children Act 1989 and Family Support: Principles into Practice.* Department of Health, HMSO.

United Nations (1989), *Conventions on the Rights of the Child,* UN.

US Dept Health Human Services (1981), *National Study of the Incidence and Severity of Child Abuse and Neglect,* DHHS Pub OHDS 81-30325.

Van Egmond, M.J. & Jonker, D. (1988), 'Sexual and physical abuse: suicide risk factors for women? The results of an empirical study amongst 158 female suicide attempters', *Tijdschrift v Psychiatrie,* 30 1 21-38.

Ward, H. & Jackson, S. (1991), 'Developing outcome measures in child care', *British Journal of Social Work,* 21 4 393-400.

Whitehead, M. (1987), *The Health Divide: Inequalities in Health in the 1980's,* Health Education Council.

W.H.O. 1973 to 1993: *Annual Statistics* World Health Organisation, Geneva.

Wilcox, R., Smith, D., Moore, J., Hewitt, A., Allan, G., Walker, H., Ropata, M., Monu, L. and Featherstone, T. (1991), *Family Decison Making: Family Group Conferences – Practioners Views,* Practitioners Publishing 1991, New Zealand. Also available from Family Rights Group London.

Zimrin, H., (1984), 'Do something: effect of human contact with the parent on abusive behaviour', *British Journal of Social Work,* 14 5 475-485.

Index